IS THERE *ANYBODY* OUT THERE?

BY

LAURA KRANTZ

A WILD THING BOOK

Abrams Books for Young Readers

New York

Cataloging-in-Publication Data has been applied for
and may be obtained from the Library of Congress.

ISBN 978-1-4197-5820-1

Text © 2023 Laura Krantz
Illustrations © 2023 Abrams Books for Young Readers
Edited by Howard W. Reeves
Illustrations and book design by Rafael Nobre

Photographs courtesy of the following: *page 8*, NASA/Bill Dunford;
page 64, NASA, ESA, CSA, STScI; *page 135*, NASA, ESA, CSA, STScI.

Printed and bound in China
10 9 8 7 6 5 4 3 2 1

Abrams Books for Young Readers are available at special discounts when
purchased in quantity for premiums and promotions as well as fundraising
or educational use. Special editions can also be created to specification. For
details, contact specialsales@abramsbooks.com or the address below.

ABRAMS The Art of Books
195 Broadway, New York, NY 10007
abramsbooks.com

To Scott, who makes my observable universe
light-years better.

And in memory of Frank Drake.
May we someday find "N."

CONTENTS

OUT OF THIS WORLD

"What is THAT?"

In October 2017, Dr. Robert Weryk stood at his desk, flipping through the stack of photos in his hand. They were of the night sky, taken by a giant telescope, and in one of them, he could see something he'd never noticed before. He looked at it more closely. Was it an asteroid? Asteroids are rocky objects that travel around the sun and are smaller than planets—they can be anywhere between hundreds of miles and tens of feet across. At first, this just looked like all the other asteroids Dr. Weryk had seen—a bright streak of light in the sky. But something about it wasn't quite right. So he grabbed a few more photos taken by the telescope on an earlier night, and he saw this thing again, in a different spot. By looking at the object's position in each photograph, from the first time it showed up until the most recent one, he was able to calculate how quickly it was moving—and, boy, was it moving FAST. A rip-roaring 196,000 miles per hour! Much faster than the average asteroid in our solar system, which travels at only about 56,000 miles per hour. That was his first clue that this object might be different from those he'd seen before.

He got his second clue when he realized that the path it had taken through our solar system wasn't normal. Most of what's in our tiny part of the galaxy is influenced by our sun's gravity, which keeps things like the planets and asteroids moving both at a predictable speed and in a predictable circle or ellipse, known as an orbit. But Dr. Weryk could tell that gravity wasn't the only thing affecting how fast this object was going. It must have already been moving at an incredible speed before it got anywhere near our sun, and because it was moving so fast, it wouldn't be trapped by our sun's gravity and forced into orbit around it.

Adding those two things together, Dr. Weryk realized that whatever it was, it had probably come from *outside* **our solar system.** That meant it was the very first time scientists had actually seen an interstellar object—an object that came from beyond our own star, the sun, and our solar system. And you better believe that this discovery made scientists, including Dr. Weryk, super excited! They had so many questions, like where had it come from? Where was it headed? And those scientists wouldn't have very much time to get all their questions answered, either. The object had already taken a sort of wide turn around the sun and was headed back out of the solar system. So they would have just a few weeks to get as much information as they could before the object disappeared from view. In fact, Dr. Weryk said, scientists almost didn't see this object at all. I'm very glad he was paying such close attention!

At this point, you might be wondering how Dr. Weryk happened to have a bunch of telescope photos on his desk. Well, you see, he has a very cool job as a planetary defense researcher. And while that might make you think he's preparing for an alien invasion, he and others like him are actually looking for asteroids that might pose a danger to Earth. To do that, they use a giant telescope known as the Pan-STARRS telescope, which sits at the tippy top of a dormant volcano known as Haleakalā Crater on the island of Maui, in Hawaii.

Pan-STARRS is an acronym that stands for <u>P</u>anoramic <u>S</u>urvey <u>T</u>elescope <u>a</u>nd <u>R</u>apid <u>R</u>esponse <u>S</u>ystem (quite a mouthful). The telescope tracks what are called near-Earth objects (NEOs)—things like asteroids, comets, or other objects that come within thirty million miles of Earth's orbit and might be on a crash course with our fragile planet. We definitely do not want a repeat of what happened sixty-six million years ago when a giant asteroid slammed into Earth and possibly helped wipe out the dinosaurs!

The telescope is one of many around the globe that are always on watch—tracking and observing potential dangers so that governments all over the world can have enough warning to take action if they do spot something. Researchers like Dr. Weryk monitor the telescopes' data, keeping an eye out for objects that are one hundred feet across or larger. One hundred feet might sound small, especially compared to how big space is, but an object that size could do some real damage because of how fast it would be moving when it hit Earth. For instance, about fifty thousand years ago, an asteroid struck what is today Arizona. Even though the asteroid was only one hundred feet wide, it destroyed all the plant life and other living things within fifteen miles in every direction! So if scientists did spot one of this size or larger, NASA's Planetary Defense Coordination Office would jump into action. That could mean sending a nuclear device that would blow up near the asteroid and change its direction. Or the office could launch a spacecraft that would slam into the asteroid and push it away from its path toward Earth. In fact, in 2022, NASA scientists successfully practiced how they would do that by crashing a probe into a harmless space rock! The good news is that right now, scientists don't see any large asteroids that might hit Earth in the next one hundred years.

Now, if you think that discovering an asteroid sounds important (and it is!), imagine finding an interstellar object, something no one on Earth had seen before—at least that they knew of—and from a place where no one on Earth has been. Astronomers—scientists who study the universe and everything in it—thought they might find interstellar objects one day, but so far, they'd never actually seen any. Until very recently, their telescopes just weren't powerful enough to see these objects, most of which never get close enough to Earth to spot. So in 2017, when this object crossed his path, Dr. Weryk was pretty excited. His friends joked that since he was the first scientist to find one, he should get to name it. An old tradition among scientists says that the first person to find something new—be it a new type of animal or plant, a planet, or an element—has the privilege of naming it. Since his first name is Robert, his friends suggested he call it the "Rob-ject" (get it?).

Thankfully, someone else came up with a much better name—'Oumuamua, which is pronounced "au-moo-uh-MOO-uh." It's an Indigenous Hawai'ian word that means "a messenger from afar, arriving first," kind of like a scout. And it definitely was arriving from afar—it had likely been traveling through the galaxy for millions of years, covering more miles than anyone can count.

Where exactly had it come from? Well, scientists don't really know for sure. It's difficult to trace its path backward because the galaxy is constantly

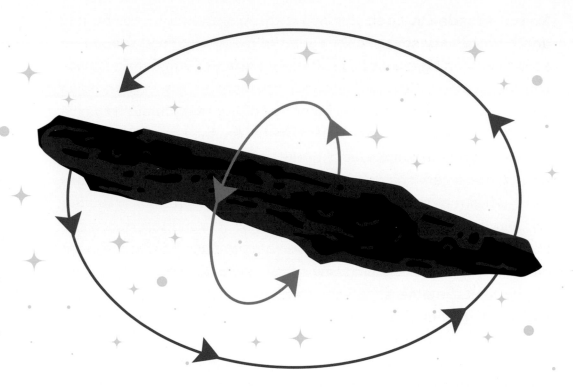

moving—and has been moving for billions of years. All they know is that it came from another star system in the galaxy. And they also don't know where it's headed—astronomers lost sight of it, even with their most advanced telescopes, in January 2018. But then there is another question that some scientists don't totally agree on: **What *is* 'Oumuamua?**

Dr. Weryk and a lot of other scientists thought it was a natural object—a rock, an asteroid, a comet—something made by nature. But another astronomer, a scientist and professor by the name of Dr. Avi Loeb, raised the possibility that maybe, just maybe, it could have been some sort of advanced technology made by aliens who are exploring the galaxy—possibly sending a scout to see what's out there.

So what made Dr. Loeb think that this object might not be just another ordinary space rock? Even the most advanced space telescopes couldn't get a clear, close-up picture of 'Oumuamua. It was too far away—a tiny, bright speck against the vast blackness of space. But even just that small pinprick of light was enough to give scientists a lot of information. For instance, they could tell that it looked really long and was shaped sort of like an éclair or a hot dog. Astronomers couldn't actually see this for themselves, but they figured it out because of how that tiny speck of light kept changing. As they looked at it from Earth, it reflected the light from our sun. Sometimes that light would look really bright, while other times it would look dim. That meant that certain sides of 'Oumuamua were bigger than the others, because they reflected so much more light, while the smaller sides looked dim, because they were reflecting less light. Bright, dim; bright, dim—this happened over and over again, which told astronomers not only that it had an unusual shape, with one side at least ten times longer than the other, but that the object was somersaulting end over end, while also spinning.

Most of the other things we've seen in space are usually more round, like a planet or a meteor, not oblong like a delicious cream-filled pastry (or a spaceship!). So that was the first piece of information that made Dr. Loeb scratch his head. It also didn't look like a comet. A comet is a small object made up of ice and dust, and when it gets close to the sun, the sun's heat turns the ice into a gas, a vapor. That vapor, along with some of the dust, becomes the tail of the comet. But as Dr. Loeb explained to me, "'Oumuamua didn't have a trail of gas and dust behind it."

An image of Comet NEOWISE from Earth shows its long tail (July 9, 2020).

ASTEROIDS VS. COMETS VS. METEORS

ASTEROIDS are the leftover bits and pieces from when our solar system first formed, about 4.6 billion years ago. These rocky objects orbit the sun and are also sometimes made of metals, like iron, and ice. The largest one we know of is about 329 miles in diameter, and the smallest is less than 33 feet. Scientists think the asteroid that may have killed the dinosaurs could have been as big as 6 miles across. There are lots of asteroids in our solar system—most of them are found in the asteroid belt, which lies between Mars and Jupiter. If you look at an asteroid through a telescope, it will look like a point of light.

COMETS are smaller than asteroids. They're made up of ice and dust, and they're mostly found way out in the solar system, beyond Neptune, where they are frozen solid. But the gravity of another planet or of the sun can sometimes cause a comet to be redirected, moving more toward the sun. Because it's made of ice, when it gets close to the sun, that ice starts to melt and boil away, turning to vapor. When you look through a telescope at a comet, you can sometimes see that vapor, along with particles of dust, streaming behind it, like a tail. Even though the comet's body is smaller than an asteroid, the tail can be millions of miles long. Then, as the comet moves away from the sun, the vapor and dust refreeze onto the comet, until the next time that it comes around.

A **METEOROID** is a small asteroid or comet, usually about the size of a pebble (although it can be a little smaller or a little bigger). When a meteoroid gets close to Earth and hits the atmosphere, it is called a **meteor**. A meteor moves very fast, but because it's so small, it burns up in the atmosphere and creates a streak of light—what we see as a shooting star. If part of a meteor survives its encounter with the atmosphere and lands on Earth, it's called a **meteorite**.

And there was one other thing. Once Dr. Weryk found 'Oumuamua in the photos taken by the telescope, scientists could make predictions about the path it would take through the solar system. Everything in our solar system follows a certain set of rules that are based on the laws of physics. Once you know how fast something is going and what direction it's headed, then you can predict where it will be in a few days or weeks and you can draw out its trajectory—its expected path of travel—on a map. So scientists did that—but 'Oumuamua kept shifting off the predicted path, and no one could understand exactly why. "It was almost like something was pushing it from behind," said Dr. Loeb.

All those things made him think differently about 'Oumuamua. He hypothesized—he made an educated guess using evidence and observations—that it might, in fact, be an object made by aliens, specifically something called a light sail. Normally we think of spacecraft as using rockets. You've probably seen movies or even watched actual launches where there's the countdown (5–4–3–2–1) and then there's liftoff, which is how the rockets propel the spacecraft into the air. The rockets have fuel inside them that burns when it's set on fire. As that fuel burns, it shoots hot gas out the back end of the rocket, and the force of that pushes the rocket (and whatever it's attached to) upward. That's great for getting your spaceship into space, but eventually you're going to run out of fuel, especially if you want to go millions of miles.

So instead of using rockets and rocket fuel, you could potentially make your spaceship move with the help of a light sail, which is a big but very thin sail that can be moved by sunlight. Light from the sun actually pushes this sail, the same way that wind pushes a sail on a ship.

I know that sounds impossible, but Dr. Loeb gave me a very good example. "When a tennis ball bounces off a wall, it gives the wall a push, a small push," he said. "Now, the building doesn't move because the building is very massive, but if you had a smaller object like another ball, then the first tennis ball would move it."

One tiny little particle of light—called a photon—couldn't push the sail on its own, but if there are lots of photons, and if the sail is thin and light enough, that sunlight could actually push it. We'll learn more about this technology in a later chapter, but it is real, and it's something that we Earthlings have just started to work on. An alien society that's more advanced than we are might have already come up with this idea. It might be sending fleets of light sails out into the universe to look for signs of life on other planets!

Of course, 'Oumuamua is now so far away that there's no way to gather evidence that might prove Dr. Loeb's idea right (or wrong). And not everyone agrees with his hypothesis. Many scientists don't even want to talk about the possibility of alien life until they know for sure that aliens actually exist. Dr. Loeb thinks that's a problem. He believes that we humans—and especially scientists—should consider the possibility that aliens might be out there.

What? **Aliens?** *Like extraterrestrials? Creatures from other galaxies and planets?* I thought when I heard this. *And they're sending spacecraft to our solar system? The same way we send spacecraft to check out other planets?*

This seems like a good moment to introduce myself. My name is Laura, and I'm a journalist. My job is to ask questions and write about what I learn for others to read. That means I get to talk to lots of interesting people who are doing cool things, like Dr. Weryk and Dr. Loeb.

Before reading all the headlines and news stories that came out after scientists found 'Oumuamua, I hadn't really spent much time thinking about extraterrestrial life. Sure, I'd seen movies about UFOs (unidentified flying objects) and heard stories about people who say they've met an alien. Maybe you have, too. Or maybe, like me, you've spent a night outside, staring up at the starry sky, wondering what might be out there. After all, space is big. Really big. Astronomical. So it's not really that weird to think that there might be other planets with other creatures living on them, right? And if we are curious about them, then it makes sense that they might be curious about us, too. So maybe it's not so strange to think that aliens flew a spacecraft through our solar system and past Earth, trying to figure out who lives here.

"I don't think that we are special or unique," Dr. Loeb told me. "We know that we exist, so looking for alien civilizations that might exist out there is a worthwhile scientific question."

Scientists aren't the only ones who ask these kinds of questions. Good journalists do, too, and after hearing everything Dr. Loeb and Dr. Weryk had to say, wow, did I have a lot of them! Could 'Oumuamua have actually been an alien spacecraft, scouting out our planet? If so, who might these aliens be, and where might they live? How would we find them, and if we did, how would we communicate with them? While there are a lot of stories about alien encounters, how do we know if any of those are true? And what does science have to say about alien life? I think that there is a good possibility that life might exist on other planets—but is it visiting us?

As I started looking into all this, one thing was certain: We couldn't rule out the possibility that 'Oumuamua was an alien spacecraft. After all, the universe isn't just big; it's huge. It's so enormous that we'll never, ever, ever be able to explore it all. And if it's so big, it wouldn't be at all surprising if something (or someone!) else is out there, in a galaxy far, far away—or maybe even right here, in ours.

ROSWELL

Let's say that somewhere out there on a faraway planet, there are living creatures that evolved into super-intelligent beings that launched a spacecraft—a spacecraft that traveled all the way to our solar system and that we named 'Oumuamua. And they've got some sort of amazing technology that we humans can't even begin to imagine: a way to travel extremely fast, not to mention avoid any collisions with bits of asteroids and other debris, while crossing the big black ocean of space. Maybe aliens are piloting that ship. Or maybe they sent an unmanned (un-aliened?) probe to take pictures and gather information, so they know which places are best to visit. What did they hope to learn from taking a trip to our little corner of the Milky Way? Were they looking specifically for us? Did they even know we existed? Do they know now? And what information did they gather about us from their flyby, if any?

'Oumuamua was not in our solar system for very long at all, so maybe the aliens weren't even interested in us! They barreled right past Earth, so maybe they had better places to be. Maybe there's so much life in the universe that Earth seems like a pretty boring planet—just one of a million others like it. Or **maybe** aliens have already visited Earth so many times over the centuries that they already know everything there is to know about us and don't even bother to stop anymore.

Another thing to think about is that Earth is 4.5 billion years old, so it's always possible that aliens came for a visit long ago, before there was even life on this planet! I can imagine a couple of aliens, Grok and Zywyskua, cruising by in their spaceship, seeing all the lava and volcanoes and poisonous gases, and deciding to take their vacation elsewhere. The review on the intergalactic version of Tripadvisor was probably along the lines of "We're giving this planet one star only because we can't give it zero."

ANCIENT VISITORS: EXTRA-TOURIST-RIALS

Some people think that lots of aliens have come to Earth over the last few thousands of years. They argue that if humans hadn't had help from aliens, we would never have been able to build some of the greatest wonders of the world. Here are a few of the most well-known:

THE PYRAMIDS OF GIZA: While Egypt has 118 known pyramids, the most famous are the Pyramids of Giza. These are the three you've mostly likely seen pictures of. The tallest, known as the Great Pyramid, is about 450 feet high and was built as a tomb for an ancient pharaoh. While we don't know exactly how the pyramids were constructed, we've found evidence of the tools that were used, including stone hammers and copper chisels. **Alien argument: There's no way that humans would have been able to move those giant, heavy stones. Also the pyramids line up with certain stars, which would have required knowing a lot about astronomy and math.**

THE NAZCA LINES: These are long lines etched into the earth in the Peruvian desert. If you look at them from far above, you can see different geometric shapes and the outlines of animals—some as big as twelve hundred feet across. Scientists think these drawings are about two thousand years old and were used for ceremonies. **Alien argument: We didn't have airplanes or drones two thousand years ago, so who would have had the ability to see these drawings from above? Aliens, of course!**

STONEHENGE: This enormous circle of stones—some of which weigh as much as one hundred thousand pounds—can be seen in the English countryside. Scientists have found that the stones are perfectly aligned with the sky during eclipses and on the summer and winter solstices—days when Earth is tilted in the farthest direction either toward the sun or away from it. These are the longest and shortest days of the year, respectively. **Alien argument: It's obviously a landing pad for alien spacecraft. And those stones would have been way too heavy for humans to move and arrange on their own.**

We don't have any scientific proof that aliens were involved in constructing these sites or providing instruction in advanced mathematics and sciences to early humans, plus there's a lot of evidence that some very advanced human civilizations built them all on their own. But it's still fun to imagine that aliens came by with some blueprints to share with us. And it's interesting to think about what else they might have helped us with. What if aliens invented pizza and brought that idea to Earth? Or told us that peanut butter and chocolate should definitely be eaten together? Maybe there's a reason that E.T. liked Reese's Pieces so much . . .

A lot of the stories about alien visitors revolve around seeing what are called underlined_unidentified underlined_flying underlined_objects—**UFOs.** There are stories about UFOs in ancient Roman records and in writings from seventeenth-century China. Strange moving lights were seen in New Zealand in 1909 and in Portugal in 1917. We don't know for sure what people saw—it could have been some sort of astronomical event, like a shooting star or an eclipse, or perhaps something weird with the weather. And there's always the possibility that it was a *different* sort of unidentified flying object—including the kind captained by aliens.

I'll admit that when I first began researching all this, I didn't know about most of these events. But there was one that I had heard of, about an object that crashed into the New Mexico desert in July 1947, outside a little town called Roswell. It's a story you might have heard, too, if you're at all interested in aliens or have wondered about UFOs.

This story is so well-known that people travel from all over the world to visit Roswell and scour the nearby desert, looking for clues. The town even holds a big festival every July to celebrate the date of the original crash. So I decided that if I wanted to know more about the details of what happened, the best thing to do would be to drive down there myself, to see what I could learn.

One of the first people I met was a man named Dennis Balthaser. He is a UFO researcher, and he's spent years reading up on all kinds of UFO sightings and talking to eyewitnesses about what they've seen.

He's done decades of research on Roswell, and he offered to tell me his version of the crash story, as we stood by a locked chain-link fence outside an old military base.

"There was a ranch about sixty-five miles northwest of here," he said. "And in July 1947, the rancher heard a sound louder than thunder—an explosion of some kind."

As Dennis said this, there was a real crack of thunder, right above us, and I jumped about a foot. While we stood there, the sky started to turn purplish black, as a thunderstorm blew in across the desert.

Oh man, *I hope it doesn't rain*, I thought. *I want to hear this story!*

Luckily, Dennis didn't even seem to notice—he just kept right on going.

"The next morning, the rancher went out to check his sheep, look at his windmills for damage, and came upon a field of debris—broken pieces of metal and wood—that stretched for three-quarters of a mile."

The rancher—whose name was William "Mac" Brazel—had no idea what this stuff was. So on July 7, he loaded some into the back of his pickup, drove to town, and gave it to the sheriff. The sheriff didn't know what it was, either, so he got in touch with an officer at the nearby Roswell Army Airfield—the old military base where Dennis and I were standing. That officer drove to Mac's ranch, picked up some more of the debris, and brought it back to the base, to see if the military could puzzle out what it was.

This is the beginning of the most famous UFO story in all ufology—the study of unidentified flying objects by people who think the objects might be aliens. There are all kinds of books, movies, and TV shows about Roswell, and everyone has different ideas about what actually happened. It's been more than seventy-five years, but people are still fascinated by this mystery. So what, exactly, did Mac find? Well, Dennis told me, on July 8, the day after the military picked up those pieces from the ranch, it informed the local newspapers and radio stations that it had captured the remains of a flying saucer—a UFO!

Of course, that news spread everywhere. And that was partly because there had been lots of stories about UFOs in the news around that time. Just a couple of weeks earlier, a pilot named Kenneth Arnold was flying near Mt. Rainier in Washington State when he saw nine shiny, round objects flying incredibly fast. He said they moved like saucers skipping on water—think of skipping a stone across a pond. When he told reporters what he'd seen, they called them "flying saucers," and the name stuck.

WHY ARE UFOS SHAPED LIKE SAUCERS?

One of the big problems with space travel is that gravity is extremely low. It might look like a lot of fun to float around inside a spaceship, but our bodies weren't really designed to do that—we need a certain amount of gravity to keep our muscles and bones strong. When astronauts return to Earth, even if they've been gone for only a few weeks, their muscles are much weaker, and it can take a while to build their bodies back up—sometimes as long as four years. If alien life exists, it most likely evolved on planets that also have gravity, so it's pretty likely that their bodies need gravity just like ours do. But space journeys are long— really long! So how is it possible to keep your body, human or alien, from wasting away in zero gravity?

We measure gravity using a unit abbreviated as G (for gravitational force or G-force). If you're standing or sitting motionless right now, your body feels the force of Earth at 1G. If you're in a car or an airplane and someone steps on the gas, the acceleration you feel that pushes you against the seat is the G-force going up. A force of 2Gs is twice the force of Earth's normal gravity, which means it will feel like you weigh twice what you normally do. If you went to Jupiter, you would experience a force of 2.5Gs, and it would be much harder to move than it is here on Earth. The G-force on the moon is 0.16Gs, which is why when you see a video of astronauts walking on the moon, they're able to take such big leaps. Space, as you've probably guessed, has very little gravity. Sometimes people say it has zero Gs, but that's not totally accurate—there is a tiny bit, known as microgravity.

What does all this have to do with the shape of UFOs? If aliens need

> gravity on their long space voyages, one way to create it is to spin a spaceship around in a circle super fast. (If you've ever been to a carnival or a fair with a ride called the "Gravitron," it's the same idea.) Of course, a disk is the best shape for something like this, and as it spins, it creates something called centrifugal force. Anyone inside gets pushed away from the center, and if it's moving at just the right rate, the centrifugal force of the spinning spaceship could simulate the gravity of just about any planet. So if alien spaceships are real, that could be one reason they look like flying saucers.

The stories that journalists wrote about Kenneth Arnold showed up in newspapers all over the country. Then, over the next couple of days, hundreds of people all around the United States and around the world also reported seeing other saucerlike objects. While the scientists and government officials who looked into some of those stories said they could be explained by weather or clouds or misidentified birds, some of the other tales left them scratching their heads. The military even started a secret program—called Project Sign—to investigate them. We'll hear more about that in a later chapter. But it's pretty clear that Americans had UFOs on the brain! So when the newspaper article about Roswell came out—and said the military claimed it had captured a flying saucer—I could see why people were extremely interested!

Dennis told me that the day after the military told the papers it had found a flying saucer, officials talked to reporters again, and **this** time they said the thing that had crashed was just a weather balloon—a big balloon that carries instruments up into the sky to measure things like temperature and humidity and to study the atmosphere.

One day, it's a UFO. The next day, it's a weather balloon. Which one is correct? At that time, people believed the weather balloon story, and all the excitement about the Roswell UFO kind of went away. But then, about thirty years later, a scientist and UFO researcher named Dr. Stanton Friedman started to wonder if maybe there was more to the story after all. Why had the military changed its story so quickly? He made a visit down to Roswell to interview some of the people who had been there when the object crashed, including a former U.S. Army major who had been one of the men picking up the debris. The man told Dr. Friedman that he didn't think it was a weather balloon. In fact, he said that whatever it was, it was "not of this world."

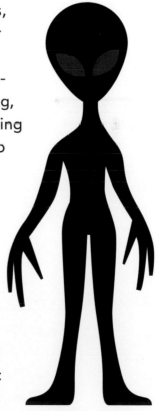

That made other UFO researchers, like Dennis, interested in coming to Roswell to start their own investigations. A couple of them wrote books, claiming that it was definitely a spaceship that had crashed after being hit by lightning, that this spaceship had technology like nothing we'd ever seen before, that the soldiers who picked up the debris also found the bodies of aliens that had died in the crash—aliens with smooth gray skin, huge heads, and large black eyes. These researchers also said the military had quietly taken those bodies first to the Roswell Army Airfield and then to another secret location to be studied. And they suggested that the government had covered up the whole thing because it didn't want Americans to panic about aliens coming to Earth. Those stories were pretty incredible, and you can see why people who read them wanted to know more!

Despite all this hubbub, the government and the military kept saying that nope, the object that crashed outside Roswell really was just a weather balloon. And then, forty-seven years later, in 1994, they changed their story again. It wasn't, in fact, a weather balloon. Instead, it was a top secret device designed to detect the kinds of sound waves made by setting off atomic bombs. The device had been part of a program called Project Mogul, and it was how we could keep an eye—well, actually, an ear—on our enemy, the Soviet Union. The reason they didn't tell people the real truth about the crash is because they wanted to keep Project Mogul a secret.

But UFO researchers didn't believe them. "The government already lied to us once," Dennis said to me. "Why would we trust them to tell the truth now?" Which raises kind of an interesting question for journalists like me and for citizens in general. We all know that sometimes the government needs to keep secrets—especially in times of war, but also when it's investigating crimes or developing new technologies. After all, it's a pretty bad idea to tell an enemy army where you plan to move your troops next or a foreign country what great new technology you're working on. But the problem with secrets is that once someone knows you're keeping them, that person might not trust anything else you say. So naturally, people might wonder what else the government might be keeping from them. Could it possibly be hiding evidence that other aliens have come to Earth? Or of some kind of amazing high-tech device found on a spacecraft that would make life better?

Of course, while I liked talking to Dennis and hearing all these wild stories about a government cover-up, the journalist in me knew we'd need real evidence—something that would prove this was some kind of alien spaceship that had been discovered in the desert and then hidden away. But none of the claims that people made about the alien bodies or amazing new technologies discovered in the crash had any proof to back them up. For example, ufologists said we got the technology for night vision (gadgets that let you see in the dark), fiber optics (a way of sending information through thin threads using light), and microchips from studying the wreckage of the crash. But it turns out we'd already started developing a lot of those technologies well before the crash, even if most people didn't know about them.

It also turned out that many of the people who said they'd witnessed something related to the Roswell incident were actually making things up. Some even went so far as to create fake evidence—like a bogus alien autopsy film and a fake diary—to try to "prove" that they'd seen the crashed UFO. Why would someone lie about something like this? Or purposefully fake evidence? It's a good question. In some cases, they might not have a very good memory of something that had happened decades before. Or they might just like the attention that comes from telling outrageous stories. Or they might be trying to make money by selling these stories or fake proof to someone who really wants to believe that aliens crashed near Roswell. Whatever the reasons, it's clear that we can't really trust a lot of the information that's out there.

There's another way to think about this—a principle called Occam's Razor, which says that you should make as few assumptions as possible (an assumption is something we accept as true without proof). Let's say there are several possible ways to explain something that happened. If we're using Occam's Razor, we'll choose the explanation that is the simplest, that requires the fewest assumptions. So let's apply this idea to the object that crashed outside Roswell. One explanation says lightning struck an alien spaceship, which crash-landed in the desert and was then recovered and hidden by the government. The other says it was actually a top secret military device.

With the alien hypothesis, we have to assume that:

1. there's life on other planets,
2. those life forms are highly evolved,
3. they have developed the kind of advanced technology they'd need to get here,
4. their spacecraft successfully navigated its way across galaxies and safely arrived at our planet, only to be struck by lightning in the last part of their trip,
5. all the aliens on board died in the crash, and
6. the government covered everything up.

That's a lot of assumptions, and they're all pretty big. Personally, I get stuck on assumption number four. I can't help but wonder why aliens would have crashed near Roswell, of all places. If they actually made it all this way to Earth, they're an incredibly powerful, technologically advanced species that was able to cross millions of miles of cold, empty space in what must have been an impossibly strong, saucer-shaped vehicle. And then, after all that, at the very last minute, a lightning storm over the desert is enough to make them crash? I'm not sure I buy it.

On the other hand, with the military device hypothesis, we have to assume that:

1. the government had a secret program,
2. the device it developed for use in this program crashed, and
3. the government kept that a secret until there was no longer a reason to worry about sharing it.

This explanation has fewer assumptions, and they're not nearly as complicated. This is a much simpler explanation and, according to Occam's Razor, the most likely one. Plus, if we think about this a little more, the military story really starts to make the most sense. The crash outside Roswell happened in 1947, which was just a couple of years after the end of World War II and at the beginning of the Cold War. The Cold War is the name we use to talk about the very tense relationship between the United States on one side and the Soviet Union on the other side. It started shortly after World War II and lasted until 1991, when the Soviet Union—formally the Union of Soviet Socialist Republics, or USSR—broke apart into smaller countries. During that time period, the United States wanted to keep a close eye on what the Soviet Union was doing—specifically with nuclear weapons. One way to do that was to listen in as the Soviets tested their

atomic bombs, using high-altitude balloons that could pick up the sound waves from the explosions, even if they were thousands of miles away. Of course, the American military didn't want the Soviets to know that we were listening, so it would have kept its program top secret, even after the device crashed. This explanation of what took place at Roswell makes a lot more sense to me than a bunch of unlucky aliens getting hit by lightning in the last leg of their long journey!

Despite all this, the name "Roswell" is practically a synonym for UFOs. The town itself is very proud of the story—the first thing you see on its main street is a giant green "Welcome to Roswell" sign with a cow being abducted by a UFO. (Why do aliens always seem to be abducting cows?) There are also alien-themed restaurants and hotels, and every July, the annual UFO festival I mentioned earlier brings in visitors from all over the country. There's even an International UFO

Museum, which is chock-full of exhibits that re-create the story of the alien crash, and right next door to that is the largest UFO research library in North America. It's packed with books, old (and no longer secret) military reports, papers from scientists, pictures, and anything else you can possibly imagine about aliens on Earth. There are even a few books on Bigfoot—for people who think Bigfoot might have been brought to this planet by aliens!

I'll admit, I was a little disappointed to realize that the Roswell crash probably didn't have anything to do with aliens—not unless someone comes up with some real proof. But there are still lots of other UFO stories out there. And here's something else that's interesting—even though the military said that what happened in Roswell had nothing to do with UFOs or aliens, it has investigated *other* possible UFO sightings. And it wasn't just doing that back in 1947. It was doing that just a few years ago. The military might even be doing that RIGHT NOW.

ALIENS OR AIRPLANES?

When Kenneth Arnold, the pilot we learned about in the last chapter, reported seeing nine objects flying near Mt. Rainier in Washington, most people believed him. After all, Kenneth seemed honest. He sure didn't act like he was making all this up. A few other people also said they'd seen the same thing that day. Then others started to report seeing UFOs and flying saucers in different places. All this made the U.S. military a little nervous. Remember, this was in 1947, and at that time, we were in the Cold War with the USSR. American officials worried that all these flying doodads people said they'd seen might actually be some kind of Soviet aircraft, one that seemed way more advanced than our own. So an American general named Nathan Twining said we should create a top secret program to look into all these UFO sightings. The military called it Project Sign. The name was later changed to Project Grudge and then finally, in 1952, to Project Blue Book.

I learned all this from Kevin Randle, a tall, mustached former officer in the U.S. Air Force, who started doing research about Project Blue Book in the 1970s. He told me that the military wanted to figure out what all these unidentified flying objects really were and if they posed any kind of threat. Basically, he said, the goal of Project Blue Book was to turn them from UFOs into IFOs, or ***identified*** flying objects.

The project lasted from 1952 all the way to 1969, and in that time, investigators collected 12,618 UFO reports from all kinds of people, especially pilots, who would often see weird things in the sky as they were flying. Sometimes it would just be one person who saw something. In some cases, *hundreds* of people would see the same strange objects in the sky.

I even have my own story that would probably have been a Project Blue Book report! When I was at summer camp one year, I saw this big green-and-red thing pulsating in the sky, early in the morning. And I wasn't the only one! A group of my friends at camp saw it, too. We were all sure it was a spaceship!

Project Blue Book's methods were pretty simple. The people working for Project Blue Book would interview anyone who claimed to have seen something, write down everything they were told, and then try to find ordinary explanations for what might have really been going on. If you've ever seen the classic TV show *The X-Files*, it's pretty similar to that. The vast majority of the Project Blue Book reports turned out to be explained by strange weather patterns, stars, funny-looking clouds, or top secret military aircraft that the public wasn't supposed to know about. Take the spaceship my friends and I thought we saw at camp, for example. We found out later that it was the planet Venus, which just happened to look super big and bright that morning.

Now, while some sightings could be easily explained, others couldn't. Kevin said that when the U.S. government finally shut down Project Blue Book in 1969, there were still about seven hundred UFOs that remained unidentified. That's seven hundred possible alien spaceships!

But after seventeen years of investigating all these sightings, military officials said they had learned all they could and they didn't want to spend time looking into UFO reports anymore. Or so they claimed. Because in 2017, we learned from newspaper stories and TV reports that, in fact, the military had had *another* secret UFO program. It was called the Advanced Aerospace Threat Identification Program, or AATIP (pronounced A-TIP), and it ran from 2007 to 2012.

Why shut down one UFO program only to create another one later? Well, even after the government officially shut down Project Blue Book, many people kept reporting that they'd seen UFOs. A lot of people. And in 2007, several powerful government officials became concerned that the military was ignoring these sightings. What if other countries were spying on us using new technology? What if our own technology was malfunctioning? And maybe less likely, but still a question, what if they *were* extraterrestrials? So these government officials established AATIP as a way to officially look into these UFO sightings, especially those by military pilots.

Now, I want you to pause and consider something for a moment: If you're a pilot flying a plane and you start saying that you see UFOs, it might make people a little nervous about flying with you.

Uh-oh, your copilots might wonder. *Are they seeing things?*

And if you're a military pilot, trained to be calm and rational, telling people you had seen weird objects flying through the air might mean your superior officers keep you from flying planes ever again!

That meant pilots kind of kept quiet about what they saw in the skies— they didn't want to lose their jobs. But that's not a very good way to try to solve a mystery. Those pilots were seeing something, even if other people didn't believe them or didn't want to hear about it. So instead of ignoring their reports, it made more sense to investigate. That's the scientific way of thinking about this!

DEFINITION OF *UFO*

Before we go any further, we should talk about the definition of *UFO*. It stands for <u>u</u>nidentified <u>f</u>lying <u>o</u>bject—any object that is flying (or appears to be) and that the person who sees it can't identify. That's it. It doesn't necessarily mean aliens. In fact, if we can for sure say it *is* aliens, or an alien spaceship, then we've identified it!

> The U.S. Air Force created the term *UFO* in the 1950s when it was trying to come up with a phrase that would cover all the various things that people reported seeing in the skies. Why not just say flying saucer? Well, the man who came up with *UFO*—Captain Edward J. Ruppelt—said that *flying saucer* was too specific and didn't cover all the possible shapes.
>
> The original definition had nothing to do with aliens, but now, when people use the term *UFO*, they often are talking about aliens. In fact, because of this, the military started using a different term—<u>u</u>nidentified <u>a</u>erial <u>p</u>henomenon, or UAP. It means the exact same thing as the original definition of *UFO*—something in the sky that we can't identify.

AATIP stayed top secret for about ten years, but then, in 2017, journalists learned about it and shared that information with the world, including some videos of strange, super-fast, and super-agile blobs (that were kind of shaped like Tic Tacs). The objects were weird. They didn't have any visible engines or anything that looked like a wing, and there wasn't any exhaust coming out of them. But based on the videos, it seemed like they could fly much faster and make tighter turns than the most advanced military jets. And because these newspaper stories and videos about UFOs and the government's secret program were now all over the internet, where everyone could find them, some of the military pilots who had seen these weird objects in the past felt more comfortable talking about what they'd seen. That included Ryan Graves, a retired U.S. Navy pilot.

I called Ryan on the phone to see if he would tell me about his experiences. He was a little nervous about discussing them because people still made fun of him for saying he'd seen UFOs when he was flying planes for the U.S. Navy—but I told him my job isn't to make fun of people, it's to ask questions and hear what they have to say. He said all these sightings—including his—started around 2014, when the U.S. Navy began upgrading all its fighter jets with a new radar system. Radar is a machine that uses radio waves (we'll learn about those in another chapter) to find faraway objects and tell how fast they're moving. After those new systems were installed, Ryan and the other pilots started seeing these weird objects on the screens in their cockpits—objects that would sometimes be holding perfectly steady in one place or would, at other times, be flying around randomly or in a racetrack pattern.

Well, you just got new systems, I thought when he told me this. *Obviously this was just a technical glitch!*

"We thought it was a technical glitch," said Ryan. They were clearly thinking the same thing I just had. "It was the most logical answer that we could come up with at the time."

The pilots saw these things all the time, anytime they were flying. They said the objects would zoom around at incredible speeds—more than 450 miles per hour—and then suddenly just stop in midair, like they were checking out something interesting. Then, without warning, they'd zoom off again, accelerating so quickly that the G-force would have been strong enough to kill a human!

At first, Ryan and the other pilots didn't think these weird things were actually real. They thought they were just software bugs in the new radar systems.

"Then some of the guys got close enough to pick it up with an optical sensor," Ryan explained.

This other sensor could detect that the flying objects were each giving off heat. While no one could make out their exact shape, Ryan said they looked like a very bright star. But if they were giving off heat, that might mean they were actual physical objects.

"That's when we started actively avoiding them when they showed up on our systems," he said. The pilots were definitely worried that they might crash into one of these mysterious objects, which would **NOT** be good.

So now everyone thought that maybe these were some kind of very advanced drone—a new technology that only people with the highest security clearance would be allowed to know about. But why would someone be testing drones near where all these pilots were practicing with their aircraft and learning the new radar system? After all, if a drone crashed into one of these very expensive military planes, it could cause major damage and possibly injure one of the pilots.

If I were flying one of those planes, I would be super curious about what might be up in the sky with me. I'd probably want to get a better look, to see if I could figure out what was going on and maybe solve this mystery once and for all. And that is exactly what these pilots wanted to do, too, Ryan said. Of course, doing so meant going really fast, just like these objects, so they'd have only a second or two to catch a glimpse. A few of them said they'd seen something, but they still didn't know for sure what it was. Another time, a couple of pilots flying side by side said one of these objects flew between their two planes. And then there was the moment when one pilot came back to base and said he'd almost had a midair collision with one. Ryan was there when the pilot returned, and he remembered the guy saying, "I almost hit one of those things!" He seemed pretty upset.

That started to make everyone nervous. What were these things? Where were they coming from? What did they want? How dangerous were they? These pilots already had a lot of things to think about while flying super-expensive equipment at monstrously fast speeds, and now they had to worry about this problem, too. But there wasn't much they could do about it. Keep in mind that this was all happening in 2014 and 2015—a time when pilots couldn't talk about UFOs without being laughed at. And even though AATIP had investigated sightings, only a handful of people were aware of that top secret program. The pilots didn't know anything about it.

Ryan and his friends weren't the first—or the last—people to see stuff like that. Stories about UFOs go back hundreds of years. More

recently, civilian pilots, military personnel, astrophysicists, airplane designers, and even a former governor of Arizona have all talked about experiences that left them scratching their heads. The former governor said he'd seen a giant triangle-shaped craft flying over a mountain range in Phoenix—and hundreds of other people said they saw the same thing, too. A U.S. Air Force colonel based in England remembered walking through a nearby forest and seeing a bright orange object with a black center, like an eye, maneuvering through the trees. At Chicago's O'Hare International Airport, dozens of people said they saw a large, disklike object floating over the runways. And these are just a handful of the sightings that have been reported in the United States and the world.

But in the past, when many of these people tried to convince others of what they'd seen or to get the government to investigate, they were ignored or, even worse, laughed at. And to be clear, many of them, including Ryan and the other pilots, weren't saying that what they saw was proof of alien life.

MEN IN BLACK AND MUFON

For years, some ufologists have traded rumors about the super-secretive (and maybe nonexistent) Men In Black—the MIB. The story goes that the MIB are part of a government agency that doesn't want anyone to know about all the aliens that are supposedly visiting Earth. So when ordinary people report seeing UFOs, they might get a visit from the MIB, who will tell them not to talk about what they've seen. Sounds like the plot to a movie, right? (It is. Four movies to be exact.)

The MIB are probably made up and are what's called a conspiracy theory—an idea that says a group of powerful people is keeping important secrets from the public. Conspiracy theories are usually pretty imaginative and sometimes more interesting than the truth. It's more entertaining to think that aliens are visiting Earth and the government is keeping it a secret—that's the whole concept behind those *Men in Black* movies. But if we really think about the evidence, it's much more likely that UFOs aren't aliens and the government isn't trying to hide anything.

But even if the MIB aren't real, there are still people to talk to if you think you have seen a UFO. They're part of an organization called MUFON—the Mutual UFO Network. It has groups all over the world and in every state in the United States. The organization was founded in 1969, around the same time that the government shut down Project Blue Book. The members of MUFON are civilians—their work with MUFON is not part of any official government or military organization—who have volunteered to interview those people who claim to have had a UFO sighting. They try to figure out if those sightings seem logical and if there's another reasonable explanation (like drones or comets or weird weather). If credible, the MUFON investigators add those stories to a big online collection, which anyone (even you!) can go look through. The website is mufon.com. This is another argument against the idea of an organization whose goal is to keep alien life secret. I think if

people were really worried about the MIB coming after them, they probably wouldn't tell anyone about what they'd seen, let alone have it published on a website!

Most of the members of MUFON are fascinated by the mystery of these objects and want to try solving it. They haven't found any answers yet—at least none that are accepted as being truly scientific—but they have collected lots of information. As one member told me, it might take hundreds of years before they figure anything out, but they're going to keep trying!

"When people hear the word *UFO*, they think of an alien spaceship," said Ryan. "I'm not saying it's that, but there was definitely something there, and we saw them every day."

It's a big jump from not being able to identify an object to assuming that the object is a ship piloted by extraterrestrials. An alien spaceship is only one possibility out of many, Ryan told me. But the bottom line is that we don't know what they are, and we should want to find out.

Dr. Avi Loeb—the astronomer who hypothesized that 'Oumuamua might be an alien probe with a light sail—said something similar: "Whatever it is, we need to find out by behaving like scientists and collecting evidence. Our prejudices get in the way. If we have the ability to detect something, then we need to contemplate all the possibilities and put them on the table and analyze them scientifically." This means that everyone—the military, the government, me, you, your family and friends—should be willing to at least consider the possibility of extraterrestrials. Of course, we have to consider all the other possibilities, too, and use evidence and science to figure out what's most likely. This means checking first to see if it might be a drone, or clouds, or a bug in the computer software, but also at least consider it could be from another planet.

As it turns out, the government *does* want to find out the truth about UFOs—that's why it started AATIP. And since then, it's created another program called the All-domain Anomaly Resolution Office (which is a not-very-exciting name for what seems like an exciting project!) to look into UFOs or UAPs. So far, it doesn't seem like that office has learned very much from its investigations, although it has said that nothing it's seen suggests aliens. My guess is the office hasn't actually found anything very interesting . . . yet.

But this isn't the only group looking into UFOs. In 2022, NASA put together a team of scientists and experts to investigate UAPs. The team will see what kind of scientific information already exists about UAPs and also try to figure out how best to study them. But like the military, NASA says there is no evidence that UAPs have anything to do with aliens.

Honestly, I think they're both telling the truth. And the reason I don't think the government is keeping secrets about alien flybys is that we don't even know for sure if there *is* other life in the universe. We've never seen any evidence of it—no space skunks or alien amoebas or extraterrestrial eels. In fact, as far as we know, the only place in the universe that has life is our own planet. But there are a lot of scientists who are looking for life out there, in our galaxy and in the ones beyond it. How on Earth **(ha!)** do they know what to look for?

WHAT IS LIFE?

What does it mean to look for alien life? Are we looking for something that's just one cell (unicellular), like an amoeba, and living in a puddle of mud on some distant planet? Or are we searching for some kind of creature that has a big brain and builds impressive alien spaceships? Would life on other planets be like life here, or completely different? And come to think of it—what exactly do we mean when we talk about life?

When I started asking around, I found out that different scientists are trying to answer this question in completely different ways. Some of them, whom we'll meet later in this book, are searching for signs of advanced alien civilizations, which include listening for radio signals in space and looking for things like air or light pollution on distant planets (which might be caused by extraterrestrial activities, just like our activities on Earth pollute the air with different things like gas, smoke, dust, and fumes, which you can actually see from space). But other scientists are starting their search at the opposite end of things, by looking for the simplest forms of life.

What is life? Well, that turns out to be a very good and very difficult question! We definitely know it when we see it, right? You and I are both examples of life, as are butterflies and slugs and giraffes and flowers. These are all considered complex organisms—they are living things with lots of different types of cells and many different parts. There's also a lot of life on Earth that we can see only with a microscope—like bacteria. These are usually made up of only one cell, or many identical cells, and are called simple organisms. The first type of life on Earth was much more closely related to those than it was to most life today.

Earth is about 4.5 billion years old, and for the first billion years or so, our planet was mostly molten rock with lots of earthquakes, toxic gases, and volcanic eruptions. Not exactly a place you'd want to live! We don't really know if anything was alive back then because most of the surface of our planet got covered in lava, so there's no fossil evidence—no preserved proof of ancient life. But evidence of ancient creatures begins appearing as fossils starting at about 3.5 billion years ago—the remains of some kind of bacteria that left impressions in rocks. We actually don't know a lot about this early life. But all life on Earth probably descended from that creature, known as the last universal common ancestor—or LUCA. We don't know what LUCA was, exactly, or what it looked like. Our best guess is that it was a single-celled organism that lived between three and four billion years ago. LUCA eventually evolved into lots of unique species. (A species is a group of organisms—for example, ginkgo trees make up one group, aardvarks another, pygmy hippopotamuses yet another—that are closely related to one another; they share similar characteristics, and they can reproduce with each other.) The first of those species would have just been simple cells, similar to bacteria. This basic form of life and the other single-celled organisms that descended from it had the planet all to themselves for almost three billion years.

It wasn't until six hundred million years ago that the first organisms with lots of cells (multicellular) started to appear in the fossil record. Then came the arthropods—the ancestors of insects and spiders, as well as creatures like lobsters and crabs. Then plants, then amphibians, and then reptiles. Mammals didn't show up until two hundred million years ago. And modern humans came along only about two hundred thousand years ago. So you can see that it took a very long time to get from those first single-celled creatures all the way up to the complex life that we easily recognize today.

EVOLUTION

The rise of new species over time happens through a process called evolution, which is a theory that explains how different types of plants and animals change over time. Basically, every time an amoeba divides in half, or an animal has babies, or a

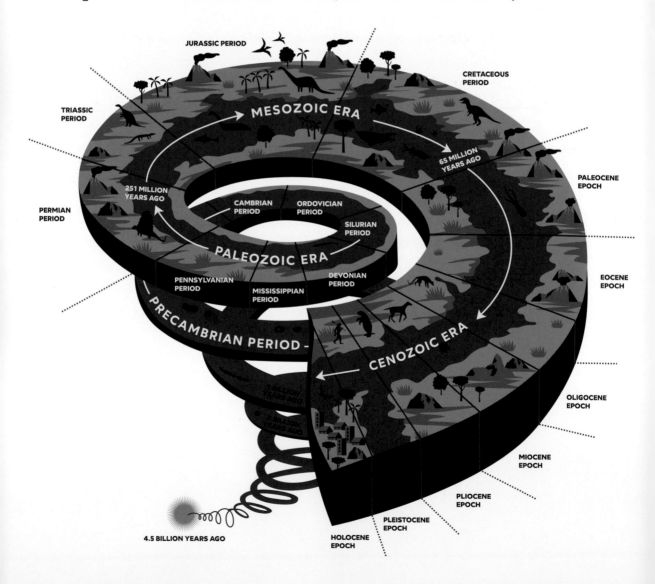

JURASSIC PERIOD

CRETACEOUS PERIOD

TRIASSIC PERIOD

MESOZOIC ERA

251 MILLION YEARS AGO

65 MILLION YEARS AGO

PALEOCENE EPOCH

PERMIAN PERIOD

CAMBRIAN PERIOD

ORDOVICIAN PERIOD

SILURIAN PERIOD

PALEOZOIC ERA

EOCENE EPOCH

PENNSYLVANIAN PERIOD

MISSISSIPPIAN PERIOD

DEVONIAN PERIOD

PRECAMBRIAN PERIOD

CENOZOIC ERA

OLIGOCENE EPOCH

MIOCENE EPOCH

PLIOCENE EPOCH

PLEISTOCENE EPOCH

4.5 BILLION YEARS AGO

HOLOCENE EPOCH

plant grows from a seed, the new generation inherits traits from its parents. Traits are characteristics, like the number of eyes an organism has or the color of its flowers. Some of those characteristics are very useful to a species and help it survive, as well as pass on those traits, generation after generation. Sometimes there might be something called a mutation that causes a small change in those traits. If that change is helpful, it can make a species even more successful!

Take the example of sea slugs. Let's say a certain species of sea slugs lives in a tide pool, and it's the only place it can live. Then a mutation occurs—a change in one of the slug's genetic makeup. Because of that mutation, some slugs will eventually develop the ability to survive not only in water but also on land very briefly. Those sea slugs are now better at moving from tide pool to tide pool, and they can find more food and better places to live. When they have baby sea slugs, it's pretty likely that those baby sea slugs will also have the same traits. After lots of generations, these sea slugs may become amphibious—meaning they can live part of their lives on land and part of them in water.

Over time, the amphibious sea slugs may no longer be in the same places as the original sea slugs. The food is different. The water temperature is different. The predators who hunt them are different. And as a result, the traits of the original sea slugs and the amphibious sea slugs become more and more different. If this goes on long enough (like thousands of years), each type of sea slug might become an entirely new creature—a new species.

Many scientists think that life in other parts of the universe would probably evolve the same way it has on Earth, starting with simple life, like those single-celled creatures, before more complex organisms could evolve over a period of millions or billions of years. In fact, on Earth, there are way more of those simple organisms than there are complex ones. So it seems likely that most of the extraterrestrial life out there in the universe would also be microscopic—more like bacteria than Marvin the Martian.

The big question, though, is where did life come from? First there was no life—just a hot, rocky, lava-flooded planet—and then, about a billion years later, simple, single-celled organisms showed up. But how did they get there? That is one of the big mysteries about life, and the truth is we're just not sure. Some scientists hypothesize that life got its start in some sort of tide pool, where there was a lot of motion from the waves and mixing of different minerals and chemicals. Others think it could have been in hydrothermal vents— openings in Earth's crust deep in the ocean, where extremely hot water and minerals escape. And there are some scientists who think that maybe life started on a different planet and hitchhiked to Earth on asteroids! That means everything on Earth might be descended from aliens—including you and me! This theory is called panspermia, but it still leaves us with a similar question: Even if life came to Earth from a different planet, how did life get *there*?

I wondered if creating life might be kind of like baking. If you get all the right ingredients, mix them together, make sure the temperature on the oven is right, and then give it enough time to bake but not burn, at the end of all that, you have some kind of cake, right? So . . . if you had a planet that had all the right "ingredients" (water and elements like carbon), which got mixed together really well (like in a tide pool), and the temperature was just right (not too cold, not too hot), could you create life? Scientists have actually been trying to do this, but I learned that it's not quite as simple (or delicious) as I'd hoped.

When you're baking, you probably have a recipe—a set of ingredients and directions that you know will result in a cake (hopefully, a red velvet cake with cream cheese frosting) if you follow them correctly. But we don't have a recipe for life! Scientists have been experimenting for decades, trying to understand where the most basic forms of life come from, but, so far, their attempts to create life in a laboratory haven't been successful. That means they're probably missing something—an important ingredient or a necessary step—but without an actual recipe, we don't know what that missing piece is.

But, you might be asking, why do we need to know where life comes from? Well, it's because it might help us figure out where to look for extraterrestrial life—what places have the right ingredients and the right temperatures (and whatever else it is that life needs to flourish). To look for life on other planets, we have to think about what makes a planet a place where life could start, survive, and thrive. But so far, the only place in the universe where we know for sure that life exists is right here on Earth. So what do we Earthlings need? To find that out, I paid a visit to Dr. David Brain, who is a planetary scientist (meaning he studies planets!) at the University of Colorado Boulder.

Dr. Brain—who has a great name—told me that all life on Earth needs three things.

That's it? I thought. *I figured it would be a list as long as my arm!*

The first, he said, is an energy source. Organisms need energy to grow and reproduce, and energy is also important for evolution. For Earthlings, the primary source of energy is the sun, which constantly bathes our planet in heat and light. Lots of creatures on this planet, including some types of plankton, algae, trees, flowers, grass and other plants, and even a type of sea slug, use sunlight as a way to make food, a process known as photosynthesis. The energy from the sun fuels their cells. Then herbivores eat plants and carnivores eat herbivores, and the energy that initially came from the sun gets passed up the food chain!

But light from the sun reaches only so far. "That's important to think about as we get further out into our solar system, where the light and heat from the sun can't reach," Dr. Brain told me.

Creatures on planets that are deeper in space will likely need some other kind of energy source, like chemical reactions underground, or thermal vents deep in the ocean, or the heat found in volcanoes.

The second thing that Dr. Brain said life needs is a combination of elements. An element is a substance that contains only one kind of atom. They're the building blocks of everything in the universe, and they can't be broken down into anything simpler. If we go back to our cake example, you can think of them as being like the ingredients. So, for instance, we can combine eggs, flour, butter, and sugar to get a cake. But if you combine them a little differently, or add other elements, you can make cookies. By combining elements together in different ways, you can create all kinds of things. And there are six elements that Dr. Brain said are essential to life on Earth.

"I remember them as CHNOPS—Carbon, Hydrogen, Nitrogen, Oxygen, Phosphorus, and Sulfur," said Dr. Brain. He explained that these chemical elements make up 98 percent of all living things on Earth. They help build the DNA that is the blueprint for life—the instructions for how to build all the different living things on Earth, which then get passed down from one generation to the next.

DNA

DNA is an acronym that stands for deoxyribonucleic acid, and one way to think about it is like a book of blueprints for what makes everything unique. Your "book" is organized into super-long chapters with instructions for different parts of the body. These chapters are called genes. One gene might tell the body how to build a tongue, while another one will have instructions for hair. The book is written in a language that uses chemical letters, called bases. Unlike an actual book in English, which is written with the twenty-six letters of our alphabet, a DNA book has only four letters: A, T, G, and C. Those letters get used over and over again, billions of times. How the four letters—those four bases—are combined makes each book different, and the order of all those letters is what's called a sequence.

What does DNA look like? Well, think of a ladder—two straight sides with the rungs between them. Now twist that ladder into a spiral, and you have a pretty good idea of DNA's shape, also known as a double helix. The two parallel sides of the ladder are what help DNA keep its shape, and they're made up of something called the sugar-phosphate backbone. The rungs of the ladder are made up of those four letters, the bases. Each rung of the ladder is created by two bases joined together, called base pairs. A is always paired with T, and G is always paired with C. These base pairs get repeated over and over again, in a different order (or sequence), and that order is like a code that tells our cells what to do.

A human book, like yours, has about 23,000 chapters (genes) with about 3 billion letters (base pairs). And every creature is different. Bananas have about 36,000 genes and 520 million base pairs!

Finally, the third thing that all life here on Earth needs is water. Not just any water: It has to be liquid water. That is because those elements we just learned about need a medium—a substance in which they can mix together and become something more complex. On Earth, we have water in all three forms—solid (ice), gas (water vapor), and liquid. And as a liquid, water is a really good medium. It can dissolve and move nutrients around, making it easier for organisms to get to them. Earth's surface is about 71 percent water (that's why Earth looks blue from space). And, in fact, most life forms on Earth are made up of water—we humans are more than 60 percent water! But water might not be liquid elsewhere (on other planets, it might be just a solid or a gas), so scientists think that there could be other mediums on other planets.

"There might be other liquids that are more favorable for life," Dr. Brain suggested. He pointed out that one of Saturn's moons, called Titan, doesn't have liquid water, but it has other liquids that could be a good medium for CHNOPS. One of those is methane, which at room temperature here on Earth is a gas (the same kind of gas that's found in burps and farts) but at colder temperatures, like those on Titan, is a liquid.

Given everything that Dr. Brain said, it seems like we have at least part of the recipe. We know we need energy, we need certain elements, and we need a liquid medium, like water. And if those ingredients are necessary for life on Earth, scientists think they could be important

elsewhere in the universe. And the great thing is that those ingredients are EVERYWHERE. They're very common, not just on planets but even just floating around the universe!

But like I mentioned before, the only place in the galaxy where we know 100 percent for sure that life exists is on Earth. So we have to make our best guesses—our best hypotheses—about life out there based on life right here. There could be all kinds of life out in the universe, but a lot of it might be so different from us that we don't recognize it. It's already hard to search for life on other planets. Searching for life when we don't know what it looks like makes it even harder.

Dr. Brain suggested that, instead of thinking about cakes (which has made me very hungry), we should think about searching for a set of lost keys. Let's say you're walking home one night and you drop your house keys somewhere in the dark. When you go back to look for those keys, where are you going to start searching? Probably where you can see best—like under a streetlamp. That might not be where your keys are, but that's where there's light.

We can think of Earth as our streetlamp—our light. And in that light, we are surrounded by life—all sorts of plants, animals, insects, bacteria, fungi, and algae in a huge variety of shapes, sizes, and colors. There are plenty of life forms for us to study and observe, in order to figure out how they function and how they evolved.

"So I think a great place to start looking for life is by searching for the kind of life that we think developed on Earth," said Dr. Brain.

Because once we understand the things we see *under* that light (here on Earth), we can start to make some good guesses about what's *outside* the light (on other planets). Given what we know about life on Earth—and the fact that most of it is microbial—scientists are looking for signs of single-celled life. Maybe it's swimming deep in the oceans of moons around Saturn and Jupiter, or floating about the atmosphere of Venus. It could even be right next door on Mars. That's what Dr. Jennifer Glass thinks might be the case. She's both a geologist (a scientist who studies the history and makeup of Earth) and an astrobiologist (a scientist who studies life on Earth in order to search for life beyond Earth).

"If we are going to find life in our solar system, it's probably going to be microbial, maybe deep under the surface of Mars or on a cold moon of one of the larger planets," she told me with an excited sparkle in her eye.

None of those places sounds like somewhere I'd want to live. But that doesn't mean we won't find life there. Dr. Glass and other scientists have traveled all over the world looking at the weird places that microbes call home—like inside volcanoes, thermal vents at the bottom of the oceans, super-salty ponds, even deep lakes in icy Antarctica. Basically, there's almost no place in the world where we haven't found life.

"We've found microbes in the heart of nuclear reactors. We can even deep-freeze these cells and bring them back to life years or even decades later," she said. "If they can survive such harsh conditions on Earth, why not on Mars? Maybe not on the surface—that's probably too harsh—but deeper underground?"

Microbes are all over Earth. Scientists estimate that the number of species is around one TRILLION. And if you counted each microbe individually? Well, you couldn't do it—it would take way too long—like 31,709 years! But scientists think there are more individual microbes on Earth than there are stars in the universe. And, as we just learned from Dr. Glass, they are everywhere. "We have to give microorganisms a lot of credit. They can do things that we can't, and they always surprise us," she said.

In fact, it's only since the 1960s that we figured out how tough microbes are, which isn't very long ago at all. A scientist went looking for life in Yellowstone National Park and realized that there were bacteria doggy-paddling around in 175-degree Fahrenheit water, which is very, very hot. Life is clearly comfortable in places that we humans will never be—which means there are a lot of possibilities for where we might find it on other planets!

So you can see why Dr. Glass is so excited about the possibility of life on Mars, and after hearing everything she had to say about microbes, it definitely doesn't seem like a crazy idea. After all, Mars has those three things that all life needs—energy, the CHNOPS elements, and even water. We've found only ice so far—not liquid water—but Mars used to have lots of liquid water on the surface, so it's possible that there still might be some underground. Do you know what that means? Extraterrestrial life could actually be right next door, quietly eating and reproducing under the surface. And if it's there, there's a good chance that life is also in LOTS of places, not just in our solar system but throughout the universe.

That's great, you're probably thinking. *But microbes are not building spaceships and sending them out all over the place! When are we going to talk about* **those** *kinds of aliens?*

We're looking. But it's pretty unlikely that big-brained, spaceship-building aliens live in our solar system. How do we know that? Well, we probably would have seen signs of them by now. We've sent a lot of probes around nearby planets and haven't seen any evidence of advanced alien life. So that means, if they're out there, they're much farther away, making them that much harder to find. But in 1961, an astronomer by the name of Dr. Frank Drake came up with an idea of how we might go about looking for them.

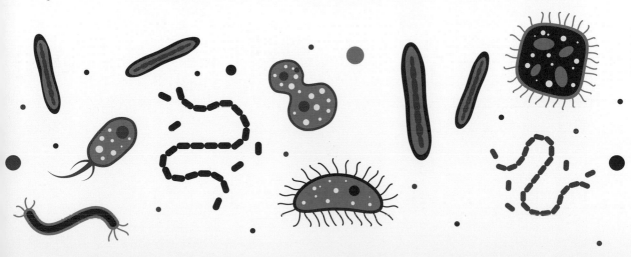

DOING SOME MATH

Get your calculators out, because we are about to use some big numbers. Huge. Absolutely enormous! I promise, you are not going to be able to use your fingers for this. So, as you probably know, we live on planet Earth, which is one of eight planets in our solar system and one of at least 100 billion planets in our galaxy—the Milky Way Galaxy. That is a lot of planets. Our galaxy also has at least that many stars and probably more. Astronomers think there could be as many as 400 billion! And that is just OUR galaxy. Do you know how many galaxies there are in the universe? That's kind of a trick question—we don't actually know for sure, because we can't see the entire universe. But based on the small part that we have seen (using two telescopes called the Hubble Space Telescope

An image from the James Webb Space Telescope as it peers through a curtain of dust and gas to reveal the birthplace of stars (July 12, 2022).

and, very recently, the James Webb Space Telescope), scientists think there are around two TRILLION galaxies out there, in what's called the observable universe—the part of space that we Earthlings can see using whatever telescopes and probes we have.

See what I mean about really big numbers?

So if we're going to go looking for alien life—whether it's itsy-bitsy microbes or more like us—we have to narrow down where we're going to look. We talked about this a little bit in the last chapter—about how you'd look for your lost keys under a streetlamp. And since we know there's life on Earth, we'd probably want to start looking for planets that are similar to Earth, because that seems like a likely spot to find life. But if there are two trillion galaxies out there, and each one of those galaxies has as many planets as ours—at least 100 billion . . . I mean, that number is so big, I don't even know where you'd start!

But back in 1961, Dr. Frank Drake came up with an idea about how to narrow down the search, especially the search for advanced aliens. Dr. Drake was an astronomer and astrophysicist—a scientist who uses physics to study how stars and planets work. I went to visit him at his house in California, and he told me about his big eureka moment.

"I realized that you would need to know how many Earths are out there, how often those Earths produced life, how often it was intelligent, and how often it made the kind of technology that we could detect with the devices we have here," Dr. Drake explained.

And that was the start of one of the most famous equations in space history—the Drake Equation. It's a formula that probably every astrophysicist, star watcher, and science fiction fan knows almost by heart.

$$N = R^* \times f_p \times n_e \times f_l \times f_i \times f_c \times L$$

"I've even had ten-year-old kids recite it to me," Dr. Drake told me with a proud smile. "They know it better than I do!"

Those ten-year-old kids are smarter than I am because, if I'm being honest, the first time I saw the equation, I wasn't sure what I was looking at. It's just a whole bunch of letters multiplied by each other! How is that going to help us get started looking for alien life? But then Dr. Drake walked me through it, and I realized that it actually makes a whole lot of sense.

On one side of the equation is **"N"**—this is what we're looking for. This is the <u>N</u>umber of civilizations we can find that we can actually communicate with. And "N" is equal to everything on the other side of the equation, starting with:

R* which is the <u>R</u>ate of <u>star</u> formation: the number of stars that are born every year. You take that number and multiply it by . . .

f$_p$ this is the <u>f</u>raction of those stars that have <u>p</u>lanets orbiting around them. Multiply that by . . .

n$_e$ for the <u>n</u>umber of planets that develop the kind of <u>e</u>cosystem that could support life. Multiple that by . . .

f$_l$ the <u>f</u>raction of those planets that actually develop <u>l</u>ife. Multiply that by . . .

f$_i$ the <u>f</u>raction of planets with life where that life becomes <u>i</u>ntelligent—it has the ability to learn, understand, use logic, and solve problems. Then you multiply that number by . . .

f$_c$ for the <u>f</u>raction of planets with intelligent life that go on to have some form of <u>c</u>ommunication. This is the number of alien civilizations that have technology we can actually see, hear, or find, like radio signals or Morse code or really bright neon lights that say "We Are Right Here!!!!" Then you take that number and multiply one more time, by . . .

L the average <u>L</u>ength of time that those signals the aliens put out can be detected.

Whew! That is a lot of multiplication! But the Drake Equation gives us a way to think about how to look for alien life and what the chances are of finding it. It's one of the reasons that Dr. Drake is known as the father of SETI—the <u>S</u>earch for <u>E</u>xtra<u>T</u>errestrial <u>I</u>ntelligence. You might have noticed that this is not the kind of equation that gives you a final answer. That's because we have ideas about only *some* of the numbers—the rest are either guesses or still big question marks. But we are learning more and more about the universe, specifically about our galaxy, and we've started to determine some real numbers that we can put into that equation.

For instance, we think that about one to three stars are formed every year. So that gives us a number for R^*. And when Dr. Drake started his career in astrophysics, we didn't know if there were planets around any stars other than our own star—the sun. But now we've actually seen them! Over the last few decades, telescopes like the Hubble Space Telescope and the Kepler Space Telescope have found thousands of these faraway planets—called exoplanets. Based on what scientists have observed, they think that, on average, every star probably has at least one planet. So that gives us a number for f_p. And the number of planets in the Milky Way that are orbiting in what's called the habitable zone—where maybe something could live, not too far from its star and not too close—could be around three hundred million! And now we have a number for n_e.

Of course, that's about as far as we can go with actual numbers, at least right now. Everything else in that equation depends on our finding life on another planet. But even without those other numbers, we know that if life exists on only a fraction of those three hundred million potentially habitable planets, that's still a lot of possibilities. One percent of three hundred million is still three million!

And you know what else? All these numbers are just based on our own galaxy—the Milky Way. When you think about what we've discovered about the rest of the universe, those numbers are absolutely enormous. That means the chances of there being life on planets other than ours are pretty darn high. Even intelligent life—whole civilizations of aliens making their own art, speaking their own languages, and building their own telescopes—seems like it's pretty likely. Especially when you think about the fact that our planet is pretty young when compared to other parts of the universe, or even our galaxy. As we learned in the last chapter, Earth is about 4.5 billion years old, and life here has likely been around for about 3.5 billion years. Modern humans have been around for only about 200,000 years. We've been building cities for only about 5,000 years. Our earliest radio signals to reach outer space (which we'll learn more about in just a second) are less than a hundred years old. So when you think about the fact that the universe is almost 14 billion years old, well, we haven't been around nearly as long. Life on older planets would have had more time to develop, which means it could be a lot more evolved and advanced than we are. Perhaps advanced enough to send an alien light sail to visit our solar system . . .

RADIO AND THE ELECTROMAGNETIC SPECTRUM

When I hear the word *radio*, I immediately think about sounds, like listening to the news or to music while I'm driving in my car. But guess what? Radio is actually a kind of light, and what's happening is that the electronics in my car stereo are taking that light and turning it into the sounds I hear.

How does THAT work? I wondered.

Thankfully, there are a lot of very smart scientists out there who can explain this, including one I'd talked to before—Dr. David Brain.

"Radio is a kind of light in the same way that visible light, the way that you and I are seeing each other right now, is a kind of light," he told me. "And there are other kinds of light: infrared, ultraviolet, X-rays, microwave—these are all different kinds of light, and radio is just one of them."

All these different kinds of light are part of something called the electromagnetic spectrum, and all of them travel at the same speed—the speed of light. But light moves like a wave, and scientists can tell the difference between the various types of light by measuring the wavelength—the difference between the peaks of the waves. The types of light that have a shorter distance between two waves are moving a lot more, which means they're more energetic. A longer distance means they're less energetic.

RADIO WAVES: These have the longest wavelength. They can range from several feet long to several miles. Their nice long wavelength make them perfect for transmitting information (like music!).

MICROWAVES: These have wavelengths that range from 0.04 inches to 12 inches. They also have a higher frequency—this is the number of wave peaks that pass by in a certain amount of time. Your microwave uses microwaves (surprise!). Microwaves specifically cause the water molecules in food to vibrate and produce heat, which is why a microwave oven is good for cooking. Microwaves are also used to send information to satellites and space probes—the size of their wavelength means they're easier to send in a specific direction.

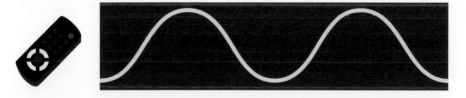

INFRARED: These wavelengths are even shorter. We can't see this light, but we can feel it as heat—like, for instance, from our sun.

VISIBLE LIGHT: This is the kind of light that can be seen by the human eye. It's emitted by the sun, and it's also how we can see things like stars, other planets, and the moon.

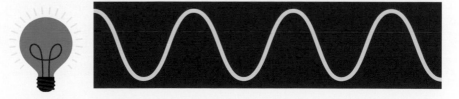

ULTRAVIOLET: This light has a shorter wavelength than visible light. We can program our telescopes to look for ultraviolet light out in the universe, letting us see faraway stars. And while this kind of light wave can't be seen by humans, it can be seen by bees. It's also emitted by the sun, and it can cause sunburn.

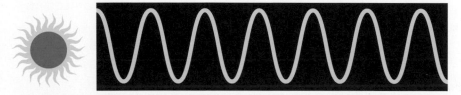

X-RAYS: These kinds of light waves are very short and very energetic—they have a very high frequency. Certain kinds of really hot stars give off light in the X-ray spectrum. Because Earth's atmosphere absorbs X-rays from space, the X-ray telescopes we use have to be at really high altitudes, even above Earth's atmosphere. X-rays can travel through solid materials, which is why they're really useful in medicine. But because they are so energetic, they can also cause damage to our cells if we're exposed to them for too long.

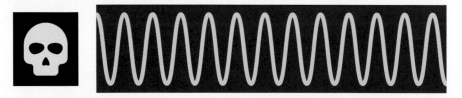

GAMMA RAYS: These are at the opposite end of the spectrum from radio waves, because they are the shortest and the most energetic. When stars explode, they release gamma rays, and we can use very special telescopes to see them. We sometimes use gamma rays to treat cancer. Like X-rays, they can travel through solid materials and also do damage to our cells.

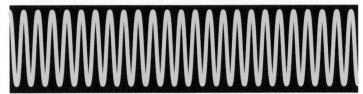

So at one end of the spectrum, we have radio waves, which have long wavelengths, low frequencies, and the lowest energy of all the different kinds of light. At the other end, we have gamma rays, which have short wavelengths, high frequencies, and the highest energy.

"Anything in this room, anything in space that you can see, by definition, has to be emitting light," explained Dr. Brain. "Anything with a temperature, which means all its atoms and molecules are moving around. Temperature is a measure of how much you're rattling around, and the more you rattle around, the more energy you're giving off. And that's what light is. Light is energy. The hotter you are, the more light you give off."

What that means is that the more energetic something is, the more light it emits (even if you can't see it). And almost everything in the universe emits some sort of light: you, me, this book, plants, and probably aliens. So why do we use radio waves to transmit information? Because they move easily through air, no matter what kind of weather we're having, and they also don't cause damage, the way fast-moving gamma rays and X-rays do!

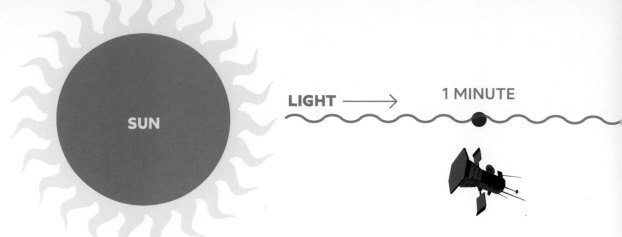

However, the age of other planets relative to ours brings up one small problem. If the aliens are so much more advanced than we are, their technology probably is, too. When Dr. Drake first dreamed up his equation, radio and television broadcasts were the best technology we had. And all those signals that were beamed around here on Earth were also beamed out in space. Anyone with the right kind of electronics could hear it. At the time, we thought this kind of technology might always be the best way to communicate, so we thought that any advanced alien civilizations out there might also be using this technology.

But technology has changed a lot since Dr. Drake first started thinking about how to look for signs of aliens. Where we once used antennas to transmit television signals, we started using cable and satellites instead. These signals are much, much quieter. You can't find them as easily, and they don't get beamed out into space the way older television and radio signals do. Earth was once a very noisy planet, sending lots of signals into space, but that's not the case anymore.

"As we're going now, within a hundred years, Earth is going to disappear" for any aliens who are trying to find our signals, Dr. Drake told me with a sigh of disappointment. He spent a good portion of his

(Continued next spread)

THE TIME IT TAKES LIGHT TO TRAVEL FROM THE SUN TO EARTH

life looking for radio signals out there in space, because he and the other scientists looking for intelligent extraterrestrials thought this would be the best way to find them. But if *we* are already becoming less noticeable after just a few decades, there's a good chance that alien signals might have done the same thing and become too quiet for us to find.

"I think radio signals are going to vanish everywhere. And that's why the most important factor in my equation is the last one—**L**—the length of time that civilizations remain detectable," he said, meaning their communication signals can be found. But these faraway alien civilizations might switch to different technology that we don't have the capability of detecting. They also might decide they don't want to be found and turn off any signals. They even might go extinct!

The other thing we have to remember is that our galaxy itself is huge, not to mention the universe, and everything is very far away. It takes a long time—sometimes thousands and even millions of years—for signals to make their way to somewhere close enough that we can detect them. We measure those distances using something called a light-year—this is the distance that light can travel in one Earth year. Shorter distances get measured in light minutes, or even light

seconds. Light travels at about 186,000 miles per second—super fast. When you flip on a light switch in your house, the flip and the resulting light seem almost instantaneous, but the truth is that the light is just traveling very fast—too fast for you to notice the time between when you flip the switch and when the light goes on. For light to travel from the sun to Earth (more than 93 million miles), it takes eight minutes. If the sun all of a sudden just turned off, we wouldn't know for eight whole minutes.

After our sun, the next-closest star to us is one called Proxima Centauri. It's almost twenty-five trillion miles away, but it takes light only about 4.2 years to travel that distance—4.2 light-years. But many stars are billions of light-years away, and while light can move pretty darn fast, the universe is so big that when that light gets to us, a lot of time has passed. So an alien civilization that is hundreds or thousands or millions of light-years away might send a signal, but by the time it gets to us, that civilization may no longer exist. It would be like if the ancient Egyptians sent out a signal into space. If some alien planet picked it up and then came looking for the ancient Egyptians, well, they're not around anymore!

Think of our radio signals as a sort of bubble expanding out in all directions from Earth. We sent the first radio signals that could

(Continued next spread)

reach outer space in the 1930s—not even 100 years ago. So that signal bubble is now about 100 light-years wide, and those signals will spread out and get fainter and harder to detect the farther they go. The Milky Way is somewhere between 100,000 and 180,000 light-years across, so those radio signals will take thousands and thousands of years to even leave our galaxy! With a really powerful radio telescope—this is a type of telescope that picks up radio waves instead of visible light waves—aimed toward Earth, alien astronomers would probably be able to pick up our signals, but they'd have to be pointing their telescopes in the right direction, and they'd also have to be close enough that those signals—the walls of our bubble—had reached them. The same is true for the astronomers on Earth who are trying to detect the radio bubbles of alien civilizations. And in the sixty years that we've been trying to find those radio signals, we haven't picked up a single transmission from outer space. Not one. That doesn't mean they're not out there; it's just that they're going to be a lot harder to find than we would like.

"People don't realize that space probably has one of the best names, because space is basically space," Dr. Jorge Perez-Gallego said, laughing. It's a play on words—*space*, meaning outer space, but also *space*, meaning a lot of room. And in outer space, there is a lot of room. "That's what we have: **space and nothingness** in between things."

VENUS

Dr. Jorge, as he likes to be called, is an astronomer and a professor. He thinks a lot about the enormous distances of space and how long it has taken the universe to form. And he wants people to understand just how far away things in space are. "We are so influenced by science fiction, and we imagine the *Millennium Falcon* [from the *Star Wars* movies] traveling at the speed of light," he said. "We imagine going from one planet in a star system to another planet in another star system in just a few seconds. But these things are waaaaay out of reach."

Everything in space is very, very far away. Remember when I said that the light from the sun takes eight minutes to get to us? And that the light from the next-nearest star, Proxima Centauri, takes more than four years? Imagine trying to have a conversation with someone living on Proxima Centauri. You'd say, **"Hello, how are you?"** and it would take four years for your message to get to them. If they replied back immediately, **"We're good—how are you?"** it would take another four years before you got your reply. That's eight years! And that's using radio waves to send messages, which can travel at the speed of light, something we humans can't yet do. If we actually wanted to visit Proxima Centauri in person? With our current technology, it would take thousands and thousands of years to get there!

8.3 MINUTES

MOON

EARTH

So you can see why looking for aliens is really, really hard. Everything in space is spread out and far away, and the farthest we humans have ever traveled is to the moon. That's still pretty far by Earth standards—it's about 238,900 miles. But remember, Proxima Centauri is close to 25 TRILLION miles away.

"Humans have not been farther away than the moon. And the solar system—just the solar system—is huge," Dr. Jorge said. "So when you start thinking about going even farther away, it's not only challenging for us but also for any other potential alien creatures that might be out there. Distances are one of the big challenges for finding extraterrestrial life!"

I started to feel a little bit **bummed** about all this. Everything is so far away, and we're not even sure exactly what we're looking for. But then I realized that the vastness of the universe also means that there are lots of places where life might be, even if we never get a chance to see it. It's worth it to keep searching, just in case, and even if we don't find life anytime soon (or ever), we might learn other interesting stuff about the universe. It turns out that a lot of scientists are thinking about this the same way and are trying to come up with cool tools that can help us look for signs of alien life—and also help us better understand space!

I SPY WITH MY LITTLE EYE

For as long as our species, *Homo sapiens*, has been around, we've been looking out into space. But until rather recently, what we've seen is only what's visible with the naked eye. It wasn't until the year 1608—just over four hundred years ago—that we invented the telescope. That first telescope wasn't nearly as powerful as the telescopes we have today—the first version only magnified objects to make them look three times larger than what we could see with our own eyes. A few years later, we'd increased that power to thirty times. But even with just that small amount, we could begin to explore our universe a little bit better. We could see that the moon wasn't the perfect smooth sphere that we'd thought it was. Instead, it had lots of mountains and craters. We saw that Jupiter had four large moons orbiting it (and later, we would discover more—scientists now think there could be as many as seventy-nine moons!). And we could see spots on the sun (creatively called "sunspots"), which ended up proving that the sun rotates (and was the first step in proving that Earth orbited the sun, rather than the other way around).

HOW DO TELESCOPES WORK?

When you hear the word *telescope*, you might think about standing in the backyard, looking through a long tube at the sky. I've done this with my dad on a clear, dark night, and we saw the rings of Saturn! His telescope is a reflecting telescope, which is a type of optical telescope, meaning it lets us see things using visible light. While it's smaller and less powerful than the reflecting telescopes that scientists use, it works the same way:

1. Light comes in the top end—the part pointed at the sky—and travels down the length of the telescope.

2. That light then bounces off a mirror that's at the back end of the telescope. This is called the primary mirror, and it's usually curved (like a shallow dish), which helps focus the light. The size of the telescope has to do with the size of

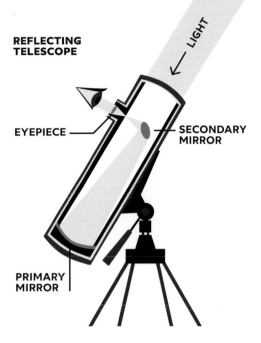

REFLECTING TELESCOPE

LIGHT

EYEPIECE

SECONDARY MIRROR

PRIMARY MIRROR

this mirror, so if someone says they have a twenty-four-inch telescope, it means the mirror at the back of the telescope is twenty-four inches in diameter (which is really big).

3. The light bounces off the primary mirror and travels back up the length of the telescope, almost to the very end, to another mirror, called the secondary mirror. It's a much smaller mirror, because the primary mirror has focused the light into a smaller path.

4. Then the light gets either reflected up into the eyepiece (for the backyard telescope) or reflected back down the telescope again, where it comes out through a small hole drilled in the primary mirror and into a camera (for scientific telescopes).

> A telescope is basically just a light-collecting bucket. Think of light as rain coming down from the sky and you want to collect as much of it as you can. The bigger your bucket (your telescope), the more light you can collect. The more light we collect, the more details we can see of something—and the newest generation of telescopes can collect a lot of light.

Those were some huge discoveries, and they happened using telescopes that, by today's standards, were fairly basic. But we've come a long way since then, and the telescope technology that's available to us now is pretty incredible. We can see so much farther, and we can look for radio signals (as we learned about earlier). We now can even launch telescopes into space, where Earth's atmosphere, which can block some of the light coming from distant objects, doesn't get in the way of things. But even with all these advances, there's still so much we can't yet see. And that's why scientists and engineers and a whole bunch of other really smart people are coming up with new ways to explore the mysteries of space and to look for signs of life. When I got a chance to talk to some of them, their ideas seemed pretty out of this world!

Right now, some of the most valuable tools we have for looking for extraterrestrial life are radio telescopes. We learned a little bit about these in the last chapter—they are telescopes that "see" radio light, rather than visible light. This is technology that we have been working with since the late 1950s. Dr. Frank Drake was one of the first scientists to use radio telescopes to look for advanced alien life, but some of the most famous SETI scientists also got their start with radio telescopes, including Dr. Jill Tarter (whose career inspired a movie about her, called *Contact*).

"An advanced technological civilization might be doing the same things—perhaps faster and better—that we do," she told me. "So we need to think about what a civilization needs, like lots of energy to power their cities and transportation to get around."

Energy and transportation are things that we need here on Earth, and from space, you can see the effects of having those things—lots of bright lights at night, especially in cities, and pollution in the atmosphere. So if aliens are doing something similar, we could look for those kinds of signs.

Or we could think about how they might communicate. Like us, an alien civilization might also be using radio transmitters—a device that sends signals using radio waves—to share information, as we talked about in the last chapter. And SETI scientists like Dr. Drake and Dr. Tarter use radio telescopes to look for those signals. They try to think of what alien civilizations might need, what they might be doing on their home worlds, and where those home worlds might be. Then they direct their radio telescopes to monitor those parts of the sky. The telescopes receive radio waves from space; then those get converted by computers into information we can study. Dr. Tarter said that while we don't know for sure that alien civilizations are using the same kind of technology that we are, it's as good a guess as any.

Now, there are lots of radio waves in space, and the vast majority of them are natural. They come from things like quasars (the super-bright centers of distant galaxies), pulsars (a type of star that spins rapidly and gives off lots of energy), and different types of gases. In fact, everything in the universe gives off radio waves, including you and me (but only a very small amount). Earth also gives off these natural radio waves, though not many of them. In fact, up until about one hundred years ago, you wouldn't be able to find Earth by using a radio telescope. But now Earth is much easier to find because of all the man-made radio waves from things like television and radio broadcasts. These artificial radio waves produce a very different kind of signal, one that we think would be pretty recognizable. So we're looking for those same types of radio waves coming from other places. Extraterrestrial places. Radio waves get transmitted on a range of frequencies (remember, this is the number of wave peaks that pass by in a certain amount of time). Radio frequencies range from 9 kilohertz to 300 gigahertz.

- One hertz is a frequency of one cycle per second—once up and once down.
- One kilohertz is a frequency of 1,000 hertz, or one thousand cycles per second.
- One megahertz is a frequency of 1 million hertz, or one million cycles per second.
- One gigahertz is a frequency of 1 billion hertz, or one billion cycles per second.

Think about that—9,000 to 300 billion is a huge range! So finding a specific signal is a little like looking for a needle in a haystack. However, keep in mind that when we first started using radio telescopes, we could listen to only one frequency at a time. Within a year, our technology had improved enough that we could listen to one thousand (using computers, of course). And now there is an international project that allows us to listen to millions of them. It's called Breakthrough Listen, and it's run by Dr. Andrew Siemion, who is an astrophysicist, like Dr. Drake. He explained to me why radio signals are such a good way to look for alien civilizations.

"Radio waves are really, really good at getting through the dust between all of the stars in our galaxy," he said. "That dust absorbs visible light, which makes it difficult to see, but radio light can go right through because it has a longer wavelength."

The Breakthrough Listen project uses radio telescopes all over the world to look for proof of extraterrestrial civilizations by looking at (actually, listening to) the one million stars that are closest to Earth, as well as one hundred nearby galaxies.

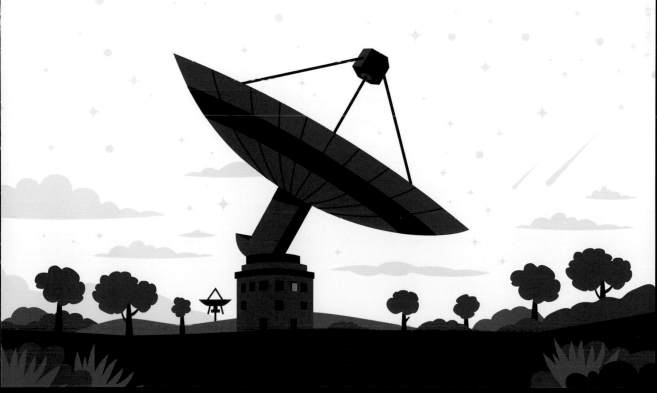

It's important to note that the signals that come from those natural sources I mentioned above (like quasars and pulsars) are kind of chaotic and random. The radio emissions that come from artificial sources, like technology, sound more orderly. So the scientists involved with Breakthrough Listen are specifically searching for radio signals that have patterns. And because these scientists are located all around the globe, they can search for a lot more of these signals than we could before.

"Whatever the chances were that we would find something ten years ago, those chances are a hundred or a thousand times better," Dr. Siemion said, with a smile on his face. "That alone gives me a lot of optimism!"

He's also optimistic because, aside from all the work being done with Breakthrough Listen, a lot of other new and powerful telescopes are being used in the search for extraterrestrial life. For example, back in 2009, NASA launched the Kepler Space Telescope on a mission to discover Earth-sized planets orbiting other stars. For a long time, scientists hypothesized that these kinds of planets existed—you might remember that this is one of the factors in the Drake Equation—but they had never had proof. For more than nine years, Kepler orbited our sun, looking only at a certain small section of the Milky Way Galaxy and then sending information about what it saw back down to Earth so scientists could

KEPLER SPACE TELESCOPE

analyze it. In total, Kepler observed 530,506 stars and found 2,662 planets.

A whole new scientific field got started—the study of exoplanets, which are planets that orbit a star other than our sun. Scientists have now confirmed that more than five thousand exoplanets exist. Not every star has a planet orbiting it—some stars have multiple planets (like our star, the sun, does)—but that still means there are potentially a lot of exoplanets. As we learned earlier, based on what we know about the number of stars out there, that could mean BILLIONS of habitable planets in the universe, some of which might have life on them.

To find out more about what scientists are learning, I called up an exoplanet expert by the name of Dr. Olivier Guyon. He's an astronomer who builds instruments that find and take images of exoplanets. He's also in charge of a project called Breakthrough Watch, which is trying to find out if any of those exoplanets are home to intelligent aliens. (And if the word *breakthrough* sounds familiar, it's because both Listen and Watch are part of a bigger space exploration program called the Breakthrough Initiatives.)

"Breakthrough Watch is looking for planets that are orbiting nearby stars, specifically planets that could be habitable and that are within twenty light-years of Earth," he told me.

"Why only twenty light-years?" I asked.

"Well, there are two reasons," he explained. "The first one is that if an exoplanet is close to us, we have better tools to study it in detail.

And the second reason is that if we get to a point where we can send probes to these planets, we want them to be near us because the travel time is so long."

Twenty light-years means it takes twenty Earth years for light (which, remember, goes 186,000 miles per second) to get from Earth to whatever planet we've picked out. No spacecraft built by humans (so far) can travel anywhere close to that fast. In fact, the fastest one we have is a probe we launched in 2018—the Parker Solar Probe—which can go as fast as 119 miles per second. That's only .064 percent of the speed of light. I'm pretty sure that one day we'll be able to create spacecraft that can go much faster, but even if we could get to 25 percent of the speed of light—46,500 miles per second—it would still take us eighty years to actually reach anything twenty light-years away! So you can see why Breakthrough Watch is starting by looking at the nearest planets.

The closest target is one we've already learned about: Alpha Centauri. Alpha Centauri is what scientists call a triple star system. Alpha Centauri A and Alpha Centauri B are two stars, similar to our sun, that orbit each other. There's also a third star, Proxima Centauri, which gets its name because it's just a tiny bit closer to us than the other two. It's a red dwarf star, meaning it has a small diameter and a lower temperature, which makes it look red. It's also not easy to see—it's not very bright, especially when we compare it with Alpha Centauri A and B, which are more like our sun.

"Proxima Centauri is personally my favorite," Dr. Guyon told me. "It's a very faint reddish star that's pretty near to us, but we can't see it with the naked eye. But it does have a rocky planet orbiting around it that could potentially be habitable."

Wait a minute, I thought. *If we can barely see Proxima Centauri, how do we know that there's a planet orbiting it? Come to think of it, how do we know any details about these exoplanets?*

Turns out, scientists are using some pretty powerful telescopes and some interesting methods to gather information about these far-flung planets and stars. In one of these methods, astronomers can look at the light coming from a star and, using a special mirror, separate that light into different colors (think of how a prism splits light into a rainbow of colors). When an exoplanet passes in front of its star,

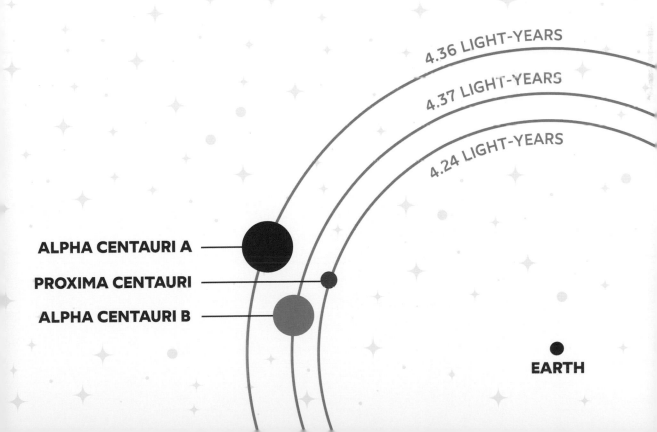

4.36 LIGHT-YEARS

4.37 LIGHT-YEARS

4.24 LIGHT-YEARS

ALPHA CENTAURI A

PROXIMA CENTAURI

ALPHA CENTAURI B

EARTH

if it has an atmosphere (like Earth), we can see the light from that faraway star passing through the exoplanet's atmosphere. As the light passes through all the gases in the atmosphere of that distant planet, the gases absorb some of the colors of light. Different colors get absorbed by different types of gases.

Here's a hypothetical example of this: Let's say the light coming from a star is made up of equal parts blue light, red light, green light, and yellow light. When we measure the light coming from the star as it passes through a planet's atmosphere, we see the same amount of blue light, red light, and yellow light, but a tiny bit less green light. Aha! Now we know that the gases in that particular atmosphere absorb green light—they keep it from escaping. And one of the gases that absorbs green light is oxygen, so there's a good chance that this atmosphere has some oxygen in it. Now, these are very small changes in color, so we can't really see them ourselves, but the computers that analyze these images sure can! This method is a type of spectroscopy, which is the study of how light interacts with matter. Spectroscopy helps us know what the atmosphere of that planet is made of, which is one of the first steps to figuring out if it's habitable.

There's another method that measures the position and motion of objects in space, and it is called astrometry, or the wobble method. Gravity plays a pretty important role in just about everything in space. The same force that keeps us standing on the surface of Earth also keeps Earth from flying out of the solar system. The easiest way to understand gravity is that every object that has mass is pulled toward every other object with mass, and the strength of that force depends on both how big the objects are and how close they are to each other. For example, we know the sun pulls planets into orbit, right? Well,

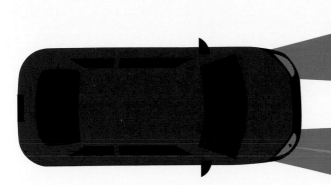

planets also pull on the sun, but because they are so much smaller, they can't pull as hard. With all that pushing and shoving, the whole system wobbles just a little bit. The wobble effect changes the color of light that we see (well, that the computer sees) from blue to red and back again—this is called the Doppler effect. If scientists see the shifting between blue and red happen regularly, it tells them that something is making that star wobble—and it's probably a planet.

There's one more method I learned about, called the transit method. Imagine if you were looking at a bright headlight on a car, and a tiny bug walked across it. You probably couldn't see that with your naked eyes, but that bug is blocking just a little bit of light. If you had a way to accurately measure the amount of light coming from the head- light, you might see that amount dip just a very small bit when the bug is crossing it. That's what our telescopes can do! When a planet passes in front of a distant sun, we can see that the light dims, ever so slightly. If the light keeps dimming and then brightening again and again, with regularity, we know there's probably a planet crossing in front of its star.

These methods are all considered *indirect* ways of detecting planets, meaning we don't actually see the planets, but the information we've gathered tells us they're there. But as our telescope technology gets better and better, we'll probably be able to see them in the future. In fact, at the end of 2021, NASA launched a new space telescope, called the James Webb Space Telescope, which we'll learn a little more about later. This telescope is in an orbit around the sun one million miles away from Earth, and it may be able to get actual photos of bigger exoplanets.

There's one other reason that the Breakthrough Watch project is focusing on nearby stars like Proxima Centauri, and that's because it's collaborating with another Breakthrough Initiative, called Breakthrough Starshot. In some ways, this might be the most exciting project of all, because its goal is to send teeny-tiny space probes to our nearest neighbors.

It sounds like it's straight out of a science fiction novel, but it's not! Remember when Dr. Avi Loeb talked about 'Oumuamua possibly being an alien light sail? A device that would use a big, thin sail that can be pushed by sunlight? That's what Breakthrough Starshot hopes to do! Dr. Pete Klupar is the chief engineer for this project, and he explained to me how it would work.

"The first goal is to shrink down the spacecraft—the probe—to get it as small as possible," he said.

The scientists and engineers working on Starshot want to make their spacecraft the size of a postage stamp so it won't require much energy to move through space. A satellite orbiting close to Earth will have thousands of these probes in it, and each probe will have a very thin sail attached to it. When the satellite sends out one of these probes, its sail will unfold to be about thirty feet by thirty feet. Think of a big umbrella but extremely thin and shiny.

But there's no wind in space! I thought. ***How will that work?***

To move the sails and the probes through space, Breakthrough Starshot will build a machine made up of lasers and mirrors that remains on Earth. The mirrors will focus the lasers into a beam of light that shoots out into space and hits the sail. That beam has so much energy that it will actually push the sail and help it accelerate to about 20 percent of the speed of light. Which means getting to Proxima Centauri, just four light-years away, will take about twenty years (instead of the thousands that it would take us to get there now).

"And then what happens?" I asked Dr. Klupar.

"Well, we'll spend about a day in that area, taking images and measurements," he said.

A day? I thought. *That's not very long at all—it just took twenty years to get there!*

There are no brakes on the probe, so it'll just whiz on by, trying to get as much information as it can to send back to Earth. The cameras probably won't be big enough to capture details like clouds, continents, or (if they're there) city lights like the ones on Earth that you can see from space—but it will give us a lot more information than we currently have.

Because the probe is so small, it won't have very powerful computers on board, either. Dr. Klupar told me it would take about a year to upload all the data it collects and then four more years to send that information back to us here on Earth (thankfully, the data can travel at the speed of light, even though the probe can't). If Dr. Loeb was right, this is the sort of mission that 'Oumuamua might have been on: a long voyage across the galaxy to gather information about a distant world, examine interesting stars, photograph unusual planets, and then send all that data back to an alien planet. It might even explain why, if 'Oumuamua *was* an alien light sail, it didn't linger very long—just like these probes, it also probably didn't have any brakes. Thinking about all that, it certainly doesn't seem like such a crazy idea, especially after I learned about Breakthrough Starshot.

They're still a long way from getting this project off the ground, but if everything goes according to plan, it would take about twenty-five years after launching the probe to get any kind of details about Proxima Centauri and its little rocky planet. Even though that seems so far away, I'm pretty excited about this mission. After all, we won't just be sending probes to Proxima Centauri to see what we can find. We'll hopefully be sending them all over the galaxy!

And it makes so much more sense to send machines to do this kind of exploration. The distances between Earth and even the closest stars make it extremely difficult to send humans. Robots don't have to worry about eating or breathing or pooping. They don't get bored (at least I don't think so). And they can last a long, long time. My fingers are crossed that Breakthrough Starshot will work and that maybe, just maybe, when you're older (and I'm really old), we might actually get to see what these probes find!

But here's another question I started to think about: If we *do* find alien life—and intelligent alien life at that—what are we going to say to them? 'Cause I'm guessing they don't speak any of the languages we have here on Earth! How do you talk to an alien?

E.T. PHONE HOME

In 1936, Earth sent out its very first radio broadcast with a signal strong enough to be found in space—the opening announcements of the 1936 Olympic Games in Berlin, Germany. Since then, that message has been traveling steadily outward, at the speed of light, into the galaxy. So any aliens flying by in their silvery space saucer, with their radio tuned to just the right spot, might catch a snippet of it (hopefully, the aliens sprechen Deutsch!). Every Earth year equals one light-year, so if you subtract the year 1936 from whatever year you're reading this, you'll know how many light-years away that radio broadcast is. In terms of distance, it's at least trillions of miles away—way farther and way faster than we humans can even dream of traveling.

That 1936 broadcast was the first of many. Over the past decades, those early radio signals grew from a trickle into a stream and then into the waterfall of broadcasts, television programs, and radar noise that currently ripple out from Earth into the universe. If any aliens are close enough and happen to be listening, they will definitely know we are here. After a while, though, and the farther out they go, those signals get fainter and fainter, and the likelihood that they'll be found goes way down. Of course, these signals came from us trying to communicate with one another and weren't really meant for alien ears (if they even have ears). If we really wanted to reach out to extraterrestrials, we'd need to deliberately send a strong signal to a place where we think there might be alien life. I was surprised to learn that we haven't really done that yet. As it turns out, some people have questioned whether this is such a good idea.

You might have heard of a physicist by the name of Dr. Stephen Hawking. He was a cosmologist—someone who studies the universe and how it's put together—and is probably one of the world's most famous and respected scientists. Although he died in 2018, his ideas have been very important to how we think about the universe and all the things in it. Dr. Hawking believed that alien life likely exists out there, somewhere, in the universe. But he worried that trying to communicate with aliens could threaten life on Earth.

"If aliens visit us, the outcome would be much as when Columbus landed in America, which didn't turn out well for the Native Americans," he once said in an interview. "We only have to look at ourselves to see how intelligent life might develop into something we wouldn't want to meet."

As he pointed out, we aren't always nice to one another—our own species—or to other species on this planet. So there's no guarantee that aliens coming from a faraway galaxy would be nice, either (and maybe they don't even know what "nice" is). Or there's the possibility that they'd want to take all our resources—like water or minerals. And if they can travel through those vast distances of space, they're probably way more advanced than we are, which would make them tough to beat in a fight. And if they are very advanced, they may see us as we see chimpanzees or ants. What if they try to use a can of ant spray (human spray?) on us?

Dr. Hawking's warning left a lot of people thinking that we should hold off on letting the aliens know where we are. But other people are less worried. For one thing, no alien civilization is likely to be very nearby, and the laws of physics are the same here as they are all over the universe. This means that aliens face the same challenges in sending spaceships to us as we do to them, so any mission would take centuries (and more likely thousands of years) and require a lot of energy. Then there's the fact that the universe is chock-full of every imaginable resource, so why would an advanced alien race even bother to come all this way to take what we have on Earth?

Personally, I hope Dr. Hawking is wrong because, in some ways, the cat is already out of the bag. As I mentioned before, we've already put lots of signals into space. And now, an organization called METI (which stands for Messaging ExtraTerrestrial Intelligence) wants to try sending messages directly to aliens—or at least to the places where we think they might be. METI is kind of the opposite of SETI. Where SETI researchers are listening for signals, METI researchers want to send powerful signals to see if we can get a response. Dr. Doug Vakoch is an astrobiologist and the president of METI, and he explained to me why he thinks we should get started sending those signals.

"There's an old saying that the best time to plant a tree was twenty years ago, and the second-best time is now," he said. "Well, the best time to send a message was twenty years ago, and the second-best time is now."

That's because, as we've already learned, it would take such a long time to get a response. As Dr. Vakoch points out, we could wait another fifty or five hundred or one thousand years, or until we think the time is right, but it'll still take forever to get a response, so we might as well just get started. Of course, we still need to figure out what we want to say, which is part of the reason that METI hasn't sent out nearly as many signals as its team might have liked.

Keep in mind that we'd have to send out a lot of messages if we hope that any extraterrestrial civilizations are going to find them. Think about it this way: If you throw only one bottle with a message in it into the ocean, it's a lot less likely to be found than if you throw lots of bottles into the ocean (although, really, it's better not to throw anything in the ocean).

So far, we've sent only a few messages. The first one went out in 1974, when scientists used the giant Arecibo radio telescope in Puerto Rico to send what's called the Arecibo Message. This message was more of a test of the telescope than an attempt to communicate

with aliens, but if any extraterrestrials do get it, it will tell them that humans do math and science, and it will give them a little bit of other information about us Earthlings. The message was written using ones and zeros—or binary code—which is how computers on Earth communicate with one another. Scientists beamed the message toward a star cluster called M13, about twenty-two thousand light-years away, which means it will get there in the year 23,974. So it's still got a looooong way to go. And, of course, there's no guarantee that aliens will be able to translate it. They probably have their own types of math and science, which might be totally different from ours. Or our binary code might look very primitive to them, and then they don't even want to talk to us because we don't seem smart enough. But, even if they don't understand us, Dr. Vakoch thinks that the message might at least give them some idea of what we're like as a civilization.

ARECIBO: A TELESCOPE AND A MESSAGE

The Arecibo Telescope was a giant radio telescope, measuring one thousand feet across. It took three years to build, and engineers constructed the telescope's bowl-shaped dish in a natural sinkhole on the island of Puerto Rico. Suspended above that dish, using a series of cables, were several radio transmitters and receivers—the instruments that scientists would use to send and receive messages. When construction finished in 1963, it was the world's biggest radio telescope, and it held that title for more than fifty years, until a bigger telescope was built in China in 2016.

Scientists used the Arecibo Telescope for radio astronomy—using radio waves to study objects in space—and made several important discoveries. For starters, they determined that the planet Mercury rotates very, very slowly—in the time it takes to rotate just once, Earth has rotated fifty-nine times. That means one Mercury Day equals fifty-nine Earth Days! They also found proof of neutron stars—the smallest and densest type of stars in the universe. And they were able to detect comets and asteroids, which made the telescope very useful in planetary defense (which, if you remember, is what

Dr. Weryk was doing when he found 'Oumuamua with the Pan-STARRS telescope).

Scientists also used the telescope to look for intelligent extra-terrestrial life, by searching for radio transmissions that might have come from advanced alien civilizations. In addition to receiving messages, they also sent one using radio waves—the famous Arecibo Message. Dr. Frank Drake, whom we met in an earlier chapter (remember the Drake Equation?), came up with this message in 1974, along with a few other scientists, including a famous astronomer named Dr. Carl Sagan. The goal was to provide any aliens who might find the message with information about Earth, like our planet's position in our solar system, and about humans, like what a human looks like and what DNA is made of.

It also included an image of the Arecibo Telescope itself. Unfortunately, even if aliens do get the message and come to Earth to see our marvelous planet, they won't be able to see the telescope that sent the message. It was damaged by hurricanes and some earthquakes, and in December 2020, the cables above the telescope's dish broke and sent the suspended instruments crashing into the dish, destroying the telescope.

A couple of years after Arecibo, in 1977, NASA launched two robotic space probes to do several flybys of Jupiter, Saturn, Uranus, and Neptune. The probes, named *Voyager I* and *Voyager II,* had an initial mission of sending information about these four planets back to Earth. They then continued on, into the outer solar system, to collect more information about things like the Kuiper Belt (another asteroid belt, beyond Neptune). Right before NASA sent the Voyagers into space, astronomer Dr. Carl Sagan came up with the idea of attaching a golden record to each probe. The discs held sounds and images that were intended to show the diversity of life and culture on Earth. If an alien stumbled across one of the probes, it could actually listen to the record (which comes with its own record player) and hear songs and nature sounds, as well as find audio signals that can be turned into pictures using computers!

After years of traveling, those *Voyager* probes crossed the final boundary of our solar system—the point where the sun's gravity no longer has any influence—and are now cruising away from our star in interstellar space (like 'Oumuamua). They're still sending information back to Earth, but scientists aren't sure how much longer the probes will work. Eventually, they won't have enough energy to keep their equipment running, but even when that happens, the probes will keep drifting farther and farther out into space. Scientists believe that in a few centuries, the probes will reach the Oort Cloud, which they think is kind of a bubble surrounding the solar system, made up of icy pieces of space debris. If you want to know where the probes are right now, you can go to their website—voyager.jpl.nasa.gov/mission/status—and get updates on both probes. As of when I wrote this book, they were both more than twelve billion miles away. And if that sounds *really* far away, guess what? It hasn't even been ONE light-year yet. In fact, the *Voyager* probes haven't even traveled an entire light-day!

So the odds are pretty low that any aliens will find them, said Dr. Sheri Wells-Jensen, who is another member of METI. "In fact, they probably won't, because space is big and the poor little *Voyager* guys are really small—but if they do, wouldn't that be great?" she exclaimed.

Dr. Wells-Jensen LOVES thinking about the Golden Records and the *Voyager* program. She teaches linguistics, which is the study of language—not just one language but languages in general, including their history and how they change over time. And the idea of sending examples of human languages out into space, where there might be other species that speak other, completely different languages, thrills her. She knows that we don't even know if there's life out there in the universe, let alone the kind of life that we might be

able to communicate with, but she really enjoys thinking about all the possibilities.

"Is anybody out there, and how are we going to find out, and what are they going to be like, and how do we get ready for them? These are some of the questions," she explained. Another question, she pointed out, is should we say hello?

"Should we put ourselves out there and say, 'Hey, guys, we're Earth, we're here, we're intelligent. Are you there? **Hello, hello, hello**—is anybody there?'"

She said that, right now, it's like we're standing around at a party, feeling awkward and lonely and wondering if anyone will ever come up and talk to us. And instead of waiting, we need to get right out there and say, "Hi, how are you?"

Just like Dr. Vakoch, she thinks that we should come up with something smart and thoughtful to say and that we should do it soon. Especially because a lot of the messages that are already out there, like from all our radio and television broadcasts, probably aren't very good. For instance, in 2008, we sent a thirty-second ad for tortilla chips up into space. In that ad, a tribe of tortilla chips sacrificed another tortilla chip to the god of salsa. I'm not sure that's the message we want to send to aliens! What kind of species will they think we are? Also, maybe they'll assume that *we* are tasty tortilla chips!

So while we want to get a message out there quickly, we also have to make sure that it's something we think aliens could decipher and that will give them an accurate picture of our planet. We're pretty sure they won't speak any Earth languages, but they might understand math and science, especially if they're able to pick up our radio signals. If they can do that, it means they must know how to build a radio receiver or a radio telescope, which means they probably think about math and physics the same way that we do.

Dr. Wells-Jensen told me to think about it this way: "Let's pretend they say, 'Beep, beep,' and then go, 'Whoop,' then say, 'Beep, beep, beep,' and then say, 'Bop. Beep, beep, beep, beep, beep.' So that's two beeps and then a funny thing and then three beeps and another funny thing and then five beeps. And one possible way to think of that is with math—the first 'whoop' means plus, and the 'bop' means equals."

Of course, we could totally get it wrong. We might be missing the point entirely. But this is our best guess, with the knowledge and information we have. And, like we learned back in an earlier chapter, the best place to look for our house keys—for answers—is where there's light, where we can see. This is why so many attempts to craft messages to aliens start by trying to make a language out of numbers. This was the idea behind the Arecibo Message and also some of what's on the Voyagers' Golden Records.

Another good reason to use math has to do with the same problem we keep running into with space—how BIG it is. Imagine that we use a radio telescope to send a message to an alien civilization that we know is two hundred light-years away, and somehow we craft it so well that the aliens speedily decode it and send their reply immediately. The round trip will take four hundred years. It's pretty hard to hold a conversation at that pace. It might take thousands of

years just to get through the basic "hellos" and "how are yous?" And during that time span, the language we're using might change a lot.

Here's an example: For a couple thousand years, no person on Earth had any idea how to read the markings in Egyptian pyramids and temples. We knew that those hieroglyphs were some sort of language, but no one could figure it out. In 1799, we got really lucky and found a stone—known as the Rosetta Stone—that had the same thing written on it in both hieroglyphs and Greek. Even with that key, it still took us more than twenty years to decipher the message. But then, once we did that, we were able to read all the other hieroglyphs.

The Egyptians stopped writing in hieroglyphs around AD 394. And since people weren't writing it anymore, they didn't feel the need to learn it, so fewer and fewer people could read it until no one could read it at all. That probably took less than one hundred years.

Or look at how much the English language has changed over time. Here are a couple of lines from *Beowulf*—a one-thousand-year-old poem written in Old English:

Hwæt! We Gardena in geardagum, þeod-cyninga þrym gefrunon, hu ða æþelingas ellen fremedon.

I'd be lying if I said that made any sense to me at all. Even when you translate it into more modern-sounding English, it's still pretty confusing:

What! We of the Spear-Danes in days-of-yore of the people-kings glory heard, how the noblemen valor did.

So think about how much a language might change between when we send a message to an extraterrestrial planet and when we get a response. By the time the aliens get back to us, our own language might have changed so much that we won't even recognize it anymore. Then we're trying to decode TWO languages—ours and the alien one! This is why math might be a better way to communicate—it doesn't change as much as other languages do, and the basic ideas remain the same. Of course, it's hard to talk about feelings or to describe the beauty of a waterfall using math.

I could see how talking to aliens could create a whole hornet's nest of problems, let alone communicating with civilizations that aren't right next door to us. And since most stars and their planets can be millions or billions of light-years away, those alien civilizations probably won't be dropping by for a visit or meeting us at the intergalactic ice cream shop anytime soon. While this might be a little disappointing, I also think it is sort of comforting. If Dr. Stephen Hawking was right about aliens wanting to conquer us, at least we know that it's probably going to take them a very long time to get to us, even if we start sending messages out into space right now.

And then there's a possibility that aliens might not use sound or even sight! Maybe they talk to each other like ants do, by passing packets of chemicals between one another; or like snakes, with smell; or maybe like elephants, who feel vibrations through the ground. In fact, thinking about all the ways that creatures here on Earth communicate with one another might give us some good ideas about how to talk to aliens. After all, some creatures here on Earth, like the ones who live deep in the trenches of the ocean or far below ground, also seem pretty alien.

An astrophysicist by the name of Dr. Laurance Doyle has been doing this kind of research with whales and dolphins, which makes a lot of sense. We know that they have huge brains, their own societies, and a way of communicating using hums, clicks, and whistles. Using a special underwater microphone called a hydrophone, Dr. Doyle recorded their sounds. He figured that if he could make at least some sense of dolphin language, we might someday in the very distant future be able to do the same with an alien language.

Dr. Doyle explained to me that scientists have found that all human languages follow a certain pattern—there are a very small number of words in every language that get used a lot, and a large number of words that don't get used very much at all. The most common word gets used twice as often as the second-most-common word and three times as often as the third-most-common word.

So let's say I spoke 20,000 words in a weekend and wrote all of them down in a little notebook. Then at the end of that weekend, I went through and counted how many times I used each word—its frequency. The word I used most often is given a rank of one. The word I used second most is given a rank of two, and so on down. This is just an example, but here's how the numbers would look for the five most common words in the English language:

1. "the" is used 2,000 times
2. "be" (including *am*, *is*, *are*, *was*, and *were*) is used half as often—1,000 times
3. "to" is used one-third as often—about 660 times
4. "of" is used one-fourth as often—roughly 500 times
5. "and" is used one-fifth as often—around 400 times

This list keeps going and going and going until you end up at words that are hardly ever used, like "meldrop," which is an old-timey word for a drop of snot and probably gets used once a century.

When scientists map this pattern out on a graph using a special mathematical formula, the line looks like a perfectly square cheese sandwich cut in half on the diagonal from the top left to the bottom right.

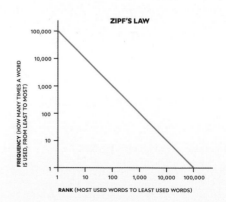

And what's cool is that this is the same in every language: Russian, Hindi, Spanish, Korean, and so on. So Dr. Doyle wanted to see if the noises that dolphins make follow that same pattern. And guess what that graph looked like? Very, very similar to the first graph, although the line is a little more crooked, and the sandwich half isn't quite a perfect triangle.

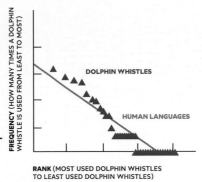

How amazing is that?!?!?! It's true that Dr. Doyle has no idea what those dolphins are saying, but he can tell that they definitely have some kind of language.

Of course, not all species do. When Dr. Doyle tried to do the same thing with squirrel monkeys and ground squirrels, it didn't work. (Similarly, I tried to map out my cats' meows, but I don't think they are speaking a language—they just want more food.) But many types of birds seem to have complex languages. In February 2020, scientists from France and Italy found that the noises made by African penguins followed the same patterns as human speech!

And even if we don't yet know what these animals are saying, Dr. Doyle thinks that these patterns might be universal—that every creature with some kind of language, including extraterrestrial creatures, will follow the same rules. Should we ever be lucky enough to get hold of an alien transmission, or the equivalent of an alien Golden Record, the research that Dr. Doyle is doing with animals could be the first step in figuring out what the aliens are saying. He's like a Dr. Dolittle for extraterrestrials!

And rather than something scary, like what Dr. Hawking imagined might happen, maybe those aliens will have a message that shares something good, like how to avoid war or how to be better galactic citizens. That's certainly what some people believe, and I wanted to find out what they hoped to learn.

DO YOU BELIEVE IN ALIENS?

The first time I ever heard about the UFO Watchtower, I was looking at an atlas of road maps as I planned a trip to New Mexico. I had been looking for routes that would have the kinds of strange roadside attractions that would make the drive more interesting. Right there on the map, about a hundred miles away from where I live in Denver, Colorado, I saw not one but two little red dots that indicated good places to check out. The first was the Colorado Gator Farm (a hot springs that is home to dozens of alligators, which is a story for another time but definitely worth a visit). And the second? The UFO Watchtower.

And, of course, if there was something called the UFO Watchtower practically in my backyard, well, I had to pay it a visit. I had so many questions. Who built it? What did they hope to find? Why build it in Colorado, of all places? Come to think of it, why build a watchtower at all? Can't you see UFOs from the ground? If I wanted answers, I knew I had to go there myself.

What I didn't know—but soon learned—was that the UFO Watchtower sits in the middle of the San Luis Valley, a place that supposedly has had more alien sightings than any other place in North America. I'd seen on the map that it was located right off the side of the highway, but honestly, even without a map, it would have been hard to miss because of the huge billboards alongside the road on the way there. The hand-lettered signs said things like **"Ride the cosmic highway to the UFO Watchtower"** and had drawings of aliens on them—including one that looked like it was riding a giant sea slug and wearing a cowboy hat. If the Watchtower wasn't already

my destination, I probably would have still stopped after seeing a sign like that one!

As I pulled up in front, I couldn't help but think that it looked like something out of *Star Wars*—a big concrete dome, like the home Luke Skywalker grew up in on Tatooine, except with more skylights. Or maybe it looked more like a giant igloo, with a big metal platform built around it (which I guessed was the "tower" part of the Watchtower). In truth, it didn't look like much of a tower. The platform was just over fifteen feet off the ground, and when I climbed up there to take a look around, I didn't feel like that extra fifteen feet made seeing UFOs any more likely.

But every year, thousands of people stop at the Watchtower to visit the shop, take pictures, walk through the garden, and climb up the stairs to get a better view. More than a few of them have said they spotted some sort of UFO—including Judy Messoline, who came up with the idea for the Watchtower in the first place.

Judy moved to the area in the 1990s with a plan to raise cattle and paint pictures of horses. But the San Luis Valley is extremely dry and very windy, and it was too hard to keep the cattle alive and healthy.

"I ran out of money, and the land wasn't good for ranching," she told me. She sold her herd—but then what? She still had all this land and needed to do *something* with it.

"From the time I moved down here, all I heard were UFO stories from the locals, and I'd just giggle and say, 'We need a UFO watchtower,'" she told me with a laugh. She just thought it would be funny. She'd never seen a UFO herself, but building a watchtower seemed like it was as good an idea as anything else she could come up with, so she built one. This idea, which she initially considered a joke, turned out to be much more interesting.

"Since I opened this in 2000, we've had 233 sightings from just here," she told me. "I've gotten to see 28 of them!"

Twenty-eight seemed like a lot. I asked her if she remembered any of them in particular. She pointed toward the mountains on the west side of the valley.

"There was one between here and the mountains—cigar-shaped, narrow, really long, and it went *zip* like that," she said as she sliced her hand through the air. "It was eleven o'clock at night. We had over a dozen people here. Everybody saw it. There was another time where we had a group of people here, and a woman jumped up just screaming, 'Do you see them? Do you see them?' Teeny-tiny dots, moving real fast toward the north. All of a sudden, the one in the front stopped, and it waited for the one behind to catch up. And when that one caught up, the two of them took off, and there was a streak of light across the sky."

When I asked her if she had any idea about what these dots—or any of the things she'd seen—might have been, she said she definitely thought some of them had perfectly reasonable explanations. The military flies its planes through this valley and probably tests out new technology here, too, which would explain why people have seen things they'd never seen before. But she doesn't think all of them are man-made.

"I really feel that there is someone from another world coming here," she told me. "I really feel that. But I don't think that they're here to harm."

I wasn't sure what to make of that. After all, we still don't have any real, convincing proof that aliens exist anywhere in the universe, let alone that they're coming to visit us here on Earth. But Judy and lots of other people have had experiences out here that they can't explain, and I did wonder what they'd seen . . . and to be honest, I was sort of hoping to have my own UFO sighting.

I figured I'd have a better chance of seeing a spaceship at night, since a dark sky would make any strange lights more obvious. Thankfully, the UFO Watchtower also allows visitors to camp overnight. But given that it was still early afternoon, I was going to have to wait a few more hours before the sun went down. So I asked Judy to give me a tour of the Watchtower in the meantime.

We started in the dome, where Judy sells Watchtower tickets and has a guest book for visitors to sign. They can also buy alien-related knickknacks like key chains, stickers, socks, action figures, and T-shirts. She also had a stash of letters that she's received over the years from visitors. My personal favorite was from a little kid who wrote to apologize for stealing a small plastic alien from the shop. "I'm so sorry for taking one extra alien from the kids' section," he wrote. "I know what I did was wrong so I am shipping it back to you. P.S. I am shipping the other alien back because I know it was wrong and I want to try and make it up to you. My brother also feels sorry so his alien is also coming back." Judy grinned as she read the letter out loud to me.

Then she pointed to what looked like a freeze-dried alien with strange stretched-out skin, packed inside an old plastic take-out container. She says that a guy from Iowa sent it to her in the mail—it was a mummified lamb he'd found in his barn that he thought looked like an alien. Super creepy—I was very glad I hadn't been the one to open that package!

We left the dome, and Judy walked me out into the garden. But this wasn't your typical garden, with green grass and trees and flowers. It looked more like a rock garden, but it was filled with all kinds of totems—items with personal meaning—that had been left behind by visitors. I saw a very random assortment of objects, like sunglasses, trophies, car parts, books, ancient Blockbuster Video membership cards, gnome statues, car keys, little green alien figurines, and just about anything that might be unearthed from a car's glove box, including hundreds and hundreds of ballpoint pens that people had stabbed into the ground.

What is all this stuff? I thought.

As if she'd read my mind, Judy explained that people who come to the Watchtower like to leave something of theirs behind, as a token to the aliens, kind of like tossing a coin into a fountain.

Why would anyone leave this stuff for aliens? I wondered. *Even if they were visiting Earth, I'm not sure these are the kinds of things aliens would want to collect!*

Judy said this practice of leaving totems started shortly after she opened the Watchtower. At first she didn't know what to make of it. She hadn't *invited* anyone to leave stuff behind; it just sort of happened. Now there are thousands, maybe tens of thousands, of small objects—some of which have important personal meaning for the people who left them. She told me that one day a family left their mother's motorcycle helmet in the garden. They said she had ridden all over the country and always used to talk about aliens. She had died in an accident, and the family felt that the best place to leave her helmet would be in the garden, a place she would have liked.

It might seem kind of strange, but, as Judy pointed out, many of the people who come here have a kind of faith in aliens—they believe in them and think they might provide some guidance for us Earthlings.

Maybe they'll have ideas on how to become better at space travel, or solve climate change, or end war, or be kinder to one another. People who feel some sort of special connection to the Watchtower see it as a place where they can ask for help or give thanks, which Judy thinks is great.

"If it helps people, it's good," she told me.

Even before Judy built the Watchtower, people were drawn to this part of the world. If you look at the history of the San Luis Valley, people have been talking about the entire area for many centuries. One Pueblo Indian legend says that their ancestors originally emerged from the hot springs that dot the region. And nearby Blanca Peak is one of the four sacred mountains of the Navajo people. So maybe, just maybe, there is something here that sets it apart from other locations. Maybe I would see something tonight after all.

The sun started to drop below the horizon and the air grew cooler, as the wind picked up. I pulled on a sweater, then a jacket and a hat, and set up my tent before it got too dark. The Watchtower closed for the night, and the few remaining visitors wandering through the garden finally left. I wasn't camping alone, thankfully. My friend Sarah Scoles had joined me, and she was kind of the perfect companion, since she'd just written a book about UFOs and spent a lot of time at the Watchtower doing research. Sarah is pretty skeptical about aliens visiting Earth, but even she had previously had a weird experience out here.

"I was looking out at the mountains, and I saw what I think people would call a classic cigar-shaped craft, just kind of this tube that was moving slowly over the land," she remembered as we sat by our campfire, the flames flickering in the wind. "I assumed it was an airplane that was aligned in a way where I couldn't see its wings. But it was strange. It's weird to see something in the sky that you don't understand."

That sighting sounded pretty similar to what Judy had described to me earlier. While Sarah didn't think it was aliens, she could understand why people might come to that conclusion. After all, you can't say for sure that aliens *aren't* out there—there's no way to prove that. The universe is so big that anything could be possible.

But what does it mean if life is all over the universe? Are we humans still significant? Or are we common and ordinary, just one of billions of other species? Humans certainly like to feel special. On Earth (where we're one species out of as many as a trillion), we tend to set ourselves apart from all the other creatures that share this planet with us. We think we're more evolved and more intelligent than just about any other animal. It could be that part of the reason people want UFOs and extraterrestrial visitors to be real is because that might make us seem special, too.

"We think we're interesting, so we think aliens should want to visit us," Sarah said.

The idea of aliens traveling to Earth suggests that we're worth making the trip for. But if life is common, if it's all over the universe, then why would aliens want to visit us here on Earth? There would be all kinds of planets to check out and solar systems to cruise through. So why here? Is it adventure tourism? Is it an opportunity to check out a less

developed planet, the same way we go to the zoo? Are we really so interesting or special that aliens are going to go out of their way to pay us a visit?

Let me use my house as an example. Right now, there are probably bugs in my basement. I know they are there even if I haven't seen them. But they aren't really worth spending a lot of time looking for because bugs are everywhere. So if bugs are common, and easily found, then why even bother looking at them? (Unless, of course, you're an entomologist—a scientist who studies bugs. Then you'd definitely want to look at them. So maybe there are aliens out there who are human-ologists or Earthling-ologists? Who are making a trip to the galaxy's basement to study us?) Maybe part of the reason we haven't seen any aliens is because we're actually pretty boring and not worth making the detour for! I mean, they can travel through space, and we've barely made it to the moon. Maybe that's why, if 'Oumuamua was an alien spacecraft, it didn't stay in our corner of the galaxy for very long—It didn't find anything it thought was interesting!

Of course, we still don't know if there is life on any planet but our own. Some scientists have even raised the question of whether Earth is the opposite of common and is actually an anomaly—something that is abnormal or unexpected. There are a lot of things about life on Earth that make it unique and potentially unlikely to be found anywhere else. This idea is called the Rare Earth Hypothesis, and it goes like this: Maybe life can emerge only on planets that have strong magnetic fields that protect it from the nearby star's radiation and that are the exact right distance away from their star, so there are fewer of those DNA-destroying cosmic rays and radiation. Maybe life can take off only on planets with large moons (just like ours) that deflect asteroids, and with big planets in the outer solar system that also help keep asteroids away. Maybe life can show up only on planets that revolve at a certain speed, with exactly the gravity that Earth has. Maybe life can exist only on planets with tectonic plates. And there are so many other maybes to consider! When you think about all the things that make Earth unique, you start to wonder how many planets actually have these same characteristics.

It could be that all the things that allowed life to evolve here *have* to happen elsewhere for life to exist there. It's like all the Drake Equation variables plus even more variables. Everything has to happen in the right place at the right time—and according to the Rare Earth Hypothesis, everything about Earth is so unique that it's the only place in the entire universe where life can exist. It's an interesting idea, but I'm not sure I believe it. Given the size of the universe, it's hard to think that Earth would be the only planet with life.

Anyway, as Sarah told me, "People think believing in UFOs makes their lives better and more interesting." What I took this to mean was that, for many people, the universe seems like a much more exciting place if there are aliens in it.

As Sarah and I talked, the sky grew darker and darker until it was finally time to climb the Watchtower's steps to look at the sky. We sat on the metal platform, gazing at the flickering pinpricks of starlight glowing above us and the Milky Way spread out overhead.

"When I am under a sky like this, I try really hard to imagine how all those tiny white lights are actual stars, just like our sun, and that all those stars have solar systems just like ours," Sarah said. "I try to imagine all of it, but it's very hard—**the universe is just so big!** Too big for my tiny brain to take it all in."

I looked up with her and also tried to think about all the stars, planets, moons, and who knows what else out there. Even though we didn't see any signs of UFOs, that was OK. I couldn't help but think that the universe is pretty amazing with or without aliens.

But I agree with Sarah that it seems awfully unlikely that our planet would be the only planet with life on it. All we have to do is find a single example of life on another planet, and then we could be pretty sure that the universe is absolutely jam-packed with living things. Scientists are working very hard to find that example, but I wondered what would happen if we don't ever answer that question? And if we don't ever know, should we still keep looking? Why is this important?

THE TRUTH IS OUT THERE

We spotted 'Oumuamua cruising through our solar system in October 2017, and it sped away silently, back into space, almost as mysteriously as it had arrived. Astronomers had only the briefest glimpse of this first known interstellar object. Using its speed, trajectory, brightness, and movement (the way it seemed to be spinning end over end), scientists developed a lot of ideas about what this object *could* be. But once it left our sun behind, there wasn't much hope of ever getting a concrete answer. So many questions remained. Was it a comet? An alien light sail? Or something we haven't yet imagined?

Then, just over two years later, an amateur astronomer in Ukraine spotted another fast-moving interstellar object. It was passing through our solar system, almost as close as 'Oumuamua did. This object—named 2I/Borisov after the man who found it—was much brighter than 'Oumuamua and had a visible tail. Astronomers immediately knew it was a comet, not an alien cruise ship. The discovery meant that interstellar objects are probably far more common than we'd even expected. Now that our telescopes are getting so much more powerful and we know what we're looking for, it seems even more likely that we'll notice these interstellar flybys.

But even though these objects might be common, 'Oumuamua itself was *still* **weird.** Its odd shape, its speed, and its movements didn't look like anything else we'd seen before or since, including 2I/Borisov. Because of that, Dr. Avi Loeb continued to argue even more forcefully that we should consider the possibility that 'Oumuamua might have been some kind of alien spacecraft, possibly one with a light sail. However, most every other astronomer disagreed.

Today, the scientific consensus—an idea that most scientists agree upon—is that 'Oumuamua is most likely an enormous chunk of ice ejected from some distant planet after a collision around a foreign star. To go back to Occam's Razor and what we learned about assumptions, it's much simpler to assume that two little planets or asteroids slammed into each other, and that some pieces flew off, than it is to say that alien civilizations are sending light sails toward Earth.

But even if 'Oumuamua isn't a spacecraft, that doesn't mean aliens aren't out there, somewhere. We've learned over and over again about how BIG space is. So even if it's hard for life to get started, even if there are lots of hurdles to its survival, the sheer number of possible places it could exist is still in the billions.

As he thought about those numbers in 1950, a very famous physicist by the name of Dr. Enrico Fermi asked a simple question while he ate lunch with his colleagues: *Where is everybody?* Given those numbers we just talked about, he wondered why we hadn't run into anybody yet. No one had found a single sign of alien intelligence—or even the most basic, one-celled version of alien life. Even now, decades later, we don't have an answer to that very frustrating question. We've improved our ability to look for life, but we still haven't seen anything. This question is called the Fermi Paradox. A paradox is a statement that is true but also seems to contradict itself. In this case, it's true that there are lots of places in the universe where aliens could possibly be *and* that we haven't seen any proof of their existence.

Of course, as we've learned, there are plenty of good reasons for why we haven't found anyone else, like the size of the universe and the time it takes to get between places. What helped me understand this even better was seeing a picture taken by the James Webb Space Telescope. In July 2022, researchers at NASA aimed Webb at a small, particularly dark patch of sky—no bigger than a grain of sand sitting on the end of your fingertip, held out at arm's length—for a little over twelve hours. Webb is so powerful that it was able to detect faint bits of infrared light that had been traveling for more than thirteen billion years. When I saw the photo, I was astonished.

Look at all those stars! I marveled. **Too many to count!**

And then I learned that those weren't just stars I was seeing but GALAXIES of stars. Lots of them. The image of this tiny patch of space contains *thousands* of galaxies. All those galaxies have millions of stars, and all those stars likely have planets around them. It's both beautiful and a little overwhelming to think about. We've only barely begun to explore our own solar system, let alone what lies beyond it, and space is so vast that there are many places we will never see, and many things we will never know.

Given all that, I understood why most people think there is alien life out there, somewhere, be it single-celled or big-brained. In fact, it seems like believing in aliens is pretty normal. And while we may not know what exactly we're searching for (or exactly where to look for it), we're better at searching now than we've ever been before.

We've come a long way since Dr. Fermi asked his lunchtime question. Since then, we've found life on Earth in places where we never thought it existed. We figured out how to send probes past the edge of our solar system. We discovered the first concrete evidence of planets around other stars. And now, not only do we know that there are likely trillions of those far-flung planets, but we can also make educated guesses about what some of them are made of. Those are huge steps on the path to discovering life elsewhere. Aliens, you better get ready, because we are coming to find you—albeit slowly!

Thousands of galaxies appear in this image taken by the James Webb Space Telescope (July 11, 2022).

JAMES WEBB AND DISCOVERIES

In the next few decades, our space-scouring technology is only going to get better. In 2021, NASA launched the James Webb Space Telescope (JWST), which I briefly mentioned earlier. It is bigger and better than anything that we've had before.

After traveling through space for about thirty days, the JWST reached its permanent home—about a million miles away from Earth. To protect the telescope's instruments and mirrors from the light and heat of our sun, it has a silvery, reflective sunshield the size of a tennis court that will always be between the telescope and the sun—kind of like the telescope is carrying a parasol.

If you've ever gone out to look at the stars at night, you know that they're easier to see if there are no lights nearby. That way, your eyes can adjust to the dark and pick up light from farther away. Similarly, the JWST needs to be in as dark a place as possible in order to collect light from distant stars, so in addition to its sunshield, it will stay in Earth's shadow.

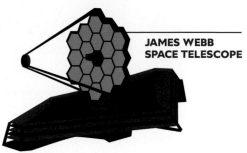

JAMES WEBB SPACE TELESCOPE

Its primary mirror is more than twenty feet across and made up of eighteen smaller mirrors arranged in a honeycomb shape. The mirrors are gold-plated so they're better at detecting light, especially in the infrared part of the spectrum, which means the telescope will be able to see farther into the universe.

The JWST will spend at least ten years—and maybe twenty, if we're lucky—looking out into space, gathering information about how the universe formed and finding new solar systems and planets. And if there are any particularly interesting planets, astronomers can learn more about their atmospheres and, just maybe, find signs of possible alien life.

It might not happen in my lifetime—or in yours. It might not happen for generations. And there's always the possibility that it might not happen ever. The universe is so big and so spread out that even if it's teeming with other types of life, we might be too far away to ever know for sure. So why do we keep looking?

In part, I think it's because if we knew who or what else was out there, we might know more about where we came from and how we evolved. We would have clues about our own past and, potentially, a glimpse into our future if the aliens we find are advanced enough. Some scientists think that, based on the age of the universe and how young

Earth is compared to other places, any alien civilization we encounter is likely going to be much older than we are. So that suggests that these aliens have figured out how to keep their civilization and planet going for a long time, which means they know how to get along with one another and their environment. They might have clues for us on how to overcome some of the problems that we face on Earth.

I also think we're looking because we like the idea that we are not alone. The possibility that Earth is the only place in the universe where life exists is a little scary, at least to me. What happens if we get hit by a giant asteroid and all life on Earth is wiped out? Then there's *no* life in the universe. At least if there are living creatures on other planets, life continues elsewhere. Being alone feels a little frightening. Finding that first evidence of extraterrestrial life would be such an exciting and important moment—knowing that we're not alone and that our planet is connected to the whole universe!

But even though we don't know for sure we'll find something, I think people will always want to keep searching. There's something about being human—maybe even something about being alive—that makes us curious about what's out there. I know I am! I look through my dad's telescope at the night sky. I think about where we could find life and what that life could be like. I wonder what all those UFO sightings might actually be. So we should keep asking questions—lots of them! We should continue to explore and discover—it's exciting to imagine all the things that we'll get to learn. And I like to think the aliens are out there and that, maybe one day, we'll actually find proof of them. The only way to do that, of course, is to keep gazing at those stars!

WHERE IS EVERYBODY?

We haven't found any signs of life yet, but here are some of the places in our own solar system we're looking!

ENCELADUS Brrrrr! Enceladus, one of Saturn's moons, is cold! It's entirely covered in ice, but occasionally, what look like huge geysers of liquid erupt from Enceladus's south pole. That means there's probably a lot of hydrothermal activity going on underneath all that ice. Hydrothermal just means heated water—and if it's heated, that means it could support life. It's going to be a while before scientists launch the Orbilander mission to look for life on Enceladus (not until 2038), but it's thrilling to think what we might find.

EUROPA Nope! Not Europe (we know there's life there). Europa is one of Jupiter's many moons. It's covered in an icy crust that might be as thick as fifteen miles. But below that, scientists think there's a giant ocean that is warm enough to be liquid, possibly because of the movement of the tides (in the same way that the moon's gravity causes tides on Earth, Jupiter's gravity causes tides on Europa). As you now know, liquid water is an important ingredient for life here on Earth. And also on Earth, we have lots of creatures living deep in our oceans. So scientists have decided that Europa is a good place to look for life, and in 2024, they're sending a spacecraft called the *Europa Clipper* to investigate. We might start getting more information about Europa in 2030, about six years after launch.

MARS   Once upon a time, billions of years ago, Mars was a lot more habitable. It had an atmosphere, like Earth has an atmosphere, to keep the temperature warm, and there were lakes and rivers of flowing water. When Mars lost its atmosphere, it became a much colder planet (it can get as cold as –220 degrees Fahrenheit at the poles during the winter!), and all that water vaporized or turned to ice. So the surface of the planet is not a great place to call home. But scientists think that if life once existed on Mars, there's a good chance it might still be there, just deep underground, where it's more protected. And they think they've found evidence of liquid water deep underground, too. NASA has sent several missions to Mars (just robots for now), to look for signs of life and learn more about our nearest neighbor!

TITAN   Another moon orbiting Saturn, Titan has lakes and rivers—but they're not flowing with water. Instead, they're made of methane! But scientists think there are also some underground oceans that could be full of water. And they know that Titan has all the ingredients that life needs—those CHNOPS elements we learned about earlier. In 2027, scientists plan to launch a mission called Dragonfly, which will reach Titan in 2034. Life on Titan isn't guaranteed, and it might be totally different from anything we've ever seen on Earth, but from everything we know already, it's definitely worth a look.

VENUS   Where Mars is cold, Venus is hot, hot, hot! The average temperature on the ground is about 847 degrees Fahrenheit—you could bake a pizza in less than two minutes (and bake yourself in the process). But while the surface of Venus might not be habitable, scientists are exploring the possibility that life could be floating around in Venus's thick atmosphere. Up in the clouds, there could be water, sunlight, and nutrients—and a much nicer temperature. Scientists plan to launch missions sometime between 2028 and 2030 to collect samples from the Venusian skies to see if there are any signs of life!

TRAPPIST-1   OK, so it's not in our solar system, but astronomers think that a group of exoplanets in a star system called TRAPPIST-1 might be an excellent place to look for life. There are seven planets there, all of them about the size of Earth, that might have temperatures just right for liquid water. TRAPPIST-1 is about thirty-nine light-years away from our sun, so we won't be going there, or sending spacecraft, anytime soon. But with the James Webb Space Telescope, we can figure out if any of these planets have an atmosphere, what those atmospheres are made of, and then possibly more about what the surfaces of those planets are like.

GLOSSARY

assumption—Something we accept as true without proof.

asteroid—A rocky object that orbits the sun.

astrobiologist—A scientist who studies life on Earth in order to search for life beyond Earth.

astrometry—Measuring the motion of objects in space.

astronomer—A scientist who studies space.

astrophysicist—A scientist who uses physics to study how stars and planets work.

binary code—A computer language written with ones and zeros.

biologist—A scientist who tries to understand the natural world and all the things that live in it.

centrifugal force—A force that causes things to move outward from the center of a rotating object.

comet—A relatively small object made up of ice and dust.

complex organisms—Living things with multiple different types of cells and many different parts.

conspiracy theory—An idea, with little or no evidence supporting it, that says a group of powerful people is keeping important secrets from the public and is acting in ways that are harmful to most other people.

cosmologist—A scientist who studies the universe and how it's put together.

debris—Scattered pieces of waste or remains.

deoxyribonucleic acid (DNA)—The parts of a cell that carry all the genetic information about how a living thing will look and function.

Drake Equation—A method of figuring out the number of extraterrestrial civilizations that we can detect.

electromagnetic spectrum—All the existing forms of light and radiation.

element—A substance that contains only one kind of atom. Elements are the building blocks of everything in the universe, and they can't be broken down into simpler chemical substances.

entomologist—A scientist who studies bugs.

evidence—An object or information showing something is true; a piece of proof.

evolution—A scientific theory that explains how living things change over time and become new species.

exoplanets—Planets that orbit a star other than our sun.

fossil—Hardened remains or traces of organisms that lived long ago.

fossil evidence—Preserved proof of ancient life, usually in stone.

frequency—How often a wave moves up and down in a certain amount of time.

G—A unit of gravity.

habitable zone—The area around a star where it is not too hot and not too cold for liquid water to exist on the surface of surrounding planets.

hydrophone—An underwater microphone.

hydrothermal vents—Openings in Earth's crust deep in the ocean, where hot water and minerals escape.

hypothesis—An educated guess that can be tested by science.

interstellar—Something from outside our solar system.

light-year—The distance that light can travel in one Earth year.

linguistics—The study of languages, including their history and how they change over time.

mass—The amount of matter an object contains.

matter—Anything that is made up of atoms and takes up space. On Earth, matter usually takes three main forms: solids, liquids, and gases.

medium—A substance in which energy and chemical elements can move around to make them more accessible.

meteor—When a meteoroid gets close to Earth and hits the atmosphere and creates a streak of light.

meteoroid—A small asteroid or comet, usually about the size of a pebble.

microbial—Relating to microbes, also called microorganisms.

microorganisms—Small living things that can't be seen with the naked eye.

Occam's Razor—A principle that says the simplest assumptions or explanations are usually more likely than complex ones.

optical telescope—A type of telescope that allows us to see objects in the visible light section of the electromagnetic spectrum.

orbit—Moving in a predictable circle or ellipse around an object.

organism—Any living thing.

panspermia—The theory that organisms such as bacteria can be transported through space to other planets on asteroids or comets.

paradox—A statement that is true but also seems to contradict itself.

photosynthesis—The process by which plants convert sunlight into food.

prejudice—An opinion that is formed without knowing or considering all the facts.

prism—A piece of glass or other see-through material with several flat sides, known as faces.

pulsars—A type of star that spins rapidly and gives off lots of energy.

quasars—The super-bright centers of distant galaxies.

radar—A machine that uses radio waves to find faraway objects and tell how fast they're moving.

radio telescope—A type of telescope that detects radio waves instead of visible light waves.

radio transmitters—A device that sends signals using radio waves.

simple organisms—Living things made up of one cell or many identical or similar cells.

solstice—When Earth is tilted in the farthest direction either toward the sun or away from it, giving us either the longest or the shortest day of the year, respectively.

spacecraft—A vehicle or machine designed to travel in space. It may or may not have people on board, and the types include probes, satellites, and space stations.

species—A group of organisms that are closely related to one another; they share similar characteristics, and they can reproduce with each other.

spectroscopy—The study of how light interacts with matter and is emitted and absorbed by different materials.

totems—Items with personal or cultural meaning.

trajectory—The expected path of a moving object.

ufology—The study of unidentified flying objects, especially by people who think they might be made by aliens.

weather balloon—A big balloon that carries instruments up into the sky to measure things like temperature and humidity and to study the atmosphere.

NOTES

INTRODUCTION: **OUT OF THIS WORLD**

1 Asteroid explainer: "Asteroid," Britannica Kids, kids.britannica.com/students /article/asteroid/272984.

2 Pan-STARRS: "Pan-STARRS Across the Sky," NASA Science, April 5, 2019, science. nasa.gov/pan-starrs-across-sky.

3 Asteroids and dinosaur extinction: See Sam Walters, "Did Volcanic Eruptions Drive the Dinosaurs to Extinction?" *Discover*, September 13, 2022, www .discovermagazine.com/the-sciences/did-volcanic-eruptions-drive-dinosaurs-to -extinction.

4 Planetary defense explainer: "Planetary Defense Coordination Office," NASA, www.nasa.gov/planetarydefense/overview.

5 Redirecting asteroids: Christian Davenport, "NASA Proved It Can Deflect an Asteroid. But Spotting Them Is Tricky," *Washington Post*, October 24, 2022, www .washingtonpost.com/technology/2022/10/24/nasa-asteroid-telescope.

6 Naming conventions: Bethan Jinkinson, "10 Species Named After Famous People," BBC News, July 19, 2012, www.bbc.com/news/magazine-18889495.

7 'Oumuamua as technology: See Shmuel Bialy and Abraham Loeb, "Could Solar Radiation Pressure Explain 'Oumuamua's Peculiar Acceleration?," *Astrophysical Journal Letters*, November 20, 2018, iopscience.iop.org /article/10.3847/2041-8213/aaeda8/pdf.

8 Description of 'Oumuamua: Elizabeth Landau, "What We Know—and Don't Know—About 'Oumuamua," NASA Science, June 27, 2018, solarsystem.nasa .gov/news/473/what-we-knowand-dont-knowabout-oumuamua.

9 Asteroid vs. comet vs. meteor: "Asteroid or Meteor: What's the Difference?," NASA Science, spaceplace.nasa.gov/asteroid-or-meteor/en.

CHAPTER 1: **ROSWELL**

17 Egyptian pyramids: Sebastian Maydana, "Egyptian Pyramids That Are NOT in Giza (Top 10)," The Collector, January 20, 2022, www.thecollector.com/top -egyptian-pyramids.

17 Great Pyramid of Giza: "Pyramids of Giza," Britannica, www.britannica.com /place/Great-Pyramid-of-Giza.

18 Nazca Lines: Taylor Tobin, "6 Ancient Sites That People Are Convinced Were Built by Aliens—and Why They Probably Weren't," Insider, July 2, 2018, www .insider.com/places-people-think-aliens-built-2018-7#the-nazca-lines-1.

18 Stonehenge: Alastair Sooke, "'If People Want Stonehenge to Be a UFO Landing Site, That's Fine,'" *Telegraph* (London), January 22, 2022, www.telegraph.co.uk /art/architecture/people-want-stonehenge-ufo-landing-site-fine.

19 Ancient stories about UFOs: See Richard Stothers, "Unidentified Flying Objects in Classical Antiquity," *Classical Journal* 103, no. 1 (2007): 79–92, www.jstor .org/stable/30038660.

19 Strange moving lights in New Zealand: Vaughan Yarwood, "X-Files: Strange Happenings in the South," *New Zealand Geographic*, July 2011, www.nzgeo .com/stories/x-files.

19 Strange moving lights in Portugal: Joaquim Fernandes and Fina d'Armada, *Celestial Secrets: The Hidden History of the Fatima Cover-up* (Charlottesville, VA: Anomalist Books, 2007).

19 Roswell incident: "Roswell Incident," Britannica, www.britannica.com/event /Roswell-incident.

22 Kenneth Arnold UFO sighting: Russell Lee, "1947: Year of the Flying Saucer," National Air and Space Museum, June 24, 2022, airandspace.si.edu/stories /editorial/1947-year-flying-saucer.

23 Astronauts and gravity: Beth Wilson, "Staying in Shape in Space," Smithsonian, November 21, 2017, airandspace.si.edu/stories/editorial/staying-shape-space.

23 Jupiter gravity: "How Strong Is the Gravity on Jupiter?," CoolCosmos, coolcosmos.ipac.caltech.edu/ask/93-How-strong-is-the-gravity-on-Jupiter.

23 Moon gravity: "Does the Moon Have Gravity?," University of Southern Maine Planetarium, usm.maine.edu/planet/does-moon-have-gravity.

23 Microgravity: "What Is Microgravity?," NASA, February 15, 2012, www.nasa.gov /audience/forstudents/5-8/features/nasa-knows/what-is-microgravity-58.html.

24 Why are UFOs shaped like saucers?: "Can Artificial Gravity Be Created in Space?," Ask an Astronomer, curious.astro.cornell.edu/about-us/150-people-in-astronomy /space-exploration-and-astronauts/general-questions/927-can-artificial -gravity-be-created-in-space-intermediate.

28 Occam's Razor: "Occam's Razor," Academic Kids Encyclopedia, academickids .com/encyclopedia/index.php/Occam%27s_Razor.

CHAPTER 2: **ALIENS OR AIRPLANES?**

34 Project Blue Book: Jonathan Marker, "Public Interest in UFOs Persists 50 Years After Project Blue Book Termination," National Archives News, December 5, 2019, www.archives.gov/news/articles/project-blue-book-50th-anniversary.

35 AATIP: Helene Cooper, Ralph Blumenthal, and Leslie Kean, "Glowing Auras and 'Black Money': The Pentagon's Mysterious U.F.O. Program," *New York Times*, December 16, 2017, www.nytimes.com/2017/12/16/us/politics/pentagon -program-ufo-harry-reid.html.

41 Former government officials and UFOs: *I Know What I Saw*, directed by James Fox, A & E Home Video, 2009.

41 O'Hare International Airport: John Keilman, "'If We're Right, It Is the Biggest Secret in History': Chicago UFO Buffs Await Release of Pentagon Report into Unexplained Sightings," *Chicago Tribune*, June 22, 2021, www.chicagotribune. com/news/breaking/ct-ufo-report-chicago-flying-objects-20210622-nre2zkt -7b5hj5ez3sb6ga4v7jq-story.html.

42 Men In Black: en.wikipedia.org/wiki/Men_in_black.

42 MUFON: See Leonard David, "UFOs Remain Elusive Despite Decades of Study," Space Insider, Space.com, June 26, 2019, www.space.com/ufo -investigations-mufon-50-years.html.

45 All-domain Anomaly Resolution Office: "DoD Announces the Establishment of the All-domain Anomaly Resolution Office," U.S. Department of Defense,

July 20, 2022, www.defense.gov/News/Releases/Release/Article/3100053
/dod-announces-the-establishment-of-the-all-domain-anomaly-resolution-office.

45 NASA and UAPs: See Katie Hunt, Ashley Strickland, and Jackie Wattles, "NASA
Announces Team of Scientists Who Will Study Mysterious 'UFO' Events in the
Sky," CNN, October 24, 2022, www.cnn.com/2022/10/24/world/ufos-nasa
-team-study-scn/index.html.

CHAPTER 3: **WHAT IS LIFE?**

48 Fossils: "Fossil," Britannica Kids, kids.britannica.com/students/article
/fossil/274394.

48 Last universal common ancestor: Keith Cooper, "Looking for LUCA, the Last
Universal Common Ancestor," NASA, March 30, 2017, astrobiology.nasa.gov
/news/looking-for-luca-the-last-universal-common-ancestor.

50 Evolution explainer: "Evolution," Britannica Kids, kids.britannica.com/students
/article/evolution/274236.

50 Geologic time scale: "Geologic Time Scale," CK–12 Foundation, updated
June 1, 2020, flexbooks.ck12.org/cbook/ck-12-middle-school-life-science-2.0
/section/4.12/primary/lesson/timeline-of-evolution-ms-ls.

54 Elements: "Chemical Element," Britannica Kids, kids.britannica.com/kids/article
/chemical-element/352942.

55 DNA explainer: "DNA," Britannica Kids, kids.britannica.com/kids/article
/DNA/390730.

56 Bananas genome: Daniel Stolte, "Mystery Peeled Off Banana Genome," University
of Arizona News, July 12, 2012, news.arizona.edu/story/mystery-peeled-off
-banana-genome.

57 60 percent water: "The Water in You: Water and the Human Body," Water
Science School, United States Geological Survey, May 22, 2019, www.usgs.gov
/special-topics/water-science-school/science/water-you-water-and-human-body.

60 One trillion species of microbes: Jay T. Lennon and Kenneth J. Locey, "There Are
More Microbial Species on Earth Than Stars in the Galaxy," *Aeon*, September
10, 2018, aeon.co/ideas/there-are-more-microbial-species-on-earth-than
-stars-in-the-sky.

60 Microbes in Yellowstone: Marybeth Shea, "Discovering Life in Yellowstone Where Nobody Thought It Could Exist," National Park Service, www.nps.gov/articles /thermophile-yell.htm.

CHAPTER 4: **DOING SOME MATH**

63 100 billion planets: "Scientists Pinpoint How Many Planets in the Milky Way Could Host Life," Inverse, October 30, 2020, www.inverse.com/science/how -many-planets-host-life.

63 400 billion stars: Maggie Masetti, "How Many Stars in the Milky Way Galaxy?," NASA, July 22, 2015, asd.gsfc.nasa.gov/blueshift/index.php/2015/07/22/how -many-stars-in-the-milky-way.

65 2 trillion galaxies: Henry Fountain, "Two Trillion Galaxies, at the Very Least," *New York Times*, October 17, 2016, www.nytimes.com/2016/10/18/science /two-trillion-galaxies-at-the-very-least.html.

69 Electromagnetic spectrum explainer: "Tour of the Electromagnetic Spectrum," NASA Science, science.nasa.gov/ems/01_intro.

70 Using radio waves to transmit information: "Electromagnetic Waves," BBC, www .bbc.co.uk/bitesize/guides/z9rqsrd/revision/2.

75 Speed of light: "Light Speed," American Museum of Natural History, www.amnh .org/explore/ology/physics/train-of-thought2/light-speed.

76 Proxima Centauri: Daniel Johnson, "Meet Proxima Centauri: The Closest Star," *Sky & Telescope*, November 30, 2021, skyandtelescope.org/astronomy-news /meet-proxima-centauri-closest-star.

79 Distance to the moon: "How Far Away Is the Moon?," Royal Museums Greenwich, www.rmg.co.uk/stories/topics/how-far-away-moon.

CHAPTER 5: **I SPY WITH MY LITTLE EYE**

81 Telescope history: "Galileo and the Telescope," Library of Congress, www.loc.gov /collections/finding-our-place-in-the-cosmos-with-carl-sagan/articles-and -essays/modeling-the-cosmos/galileo-and-the-telescope.

84 Telescope evolution: "The Evolution of the Telescope," Groovy Lab in a Box, www .groovylabinabox.com/the-evolution-of-the-telescope.

85 Radio astronomy: See Tim Stephens, "Pioneering Radio Astronomer Frank Drake Dies at 92," UC Santa Cruz Newscenter, September 2, 2022, news.ucsc .edu/2022/09/frank-drake-in-memoriam.html.

86 Hertz explainer: See "Anatomy of an Electromagnetic Wave," NASA Science, science.nasa.gov/ems/02_anatomy.

88 Kepler Space Telescope: Michele Starr, "This Is the Last Full View the Kepler Spacecraft Saw Before It Shut Down Forever," Science Alert, February 7, 2017, www.sciencealert.com/this-is-the-last-full-view-the-kepler-spacecraft-saw -before-it-shut-down-forever.

89 Five thousand exoplanets: Ethan Siegel, "Were Wrong: All Stars Don't Have Planets After All," Big Think, August 10, 2022, bigthink.com/starts-with-a-bang /stars-dont-have-planets/

89 Stars with multiple planets: Ashley Hamer, "Does Every Star Have Planets?" Live Science, December 25, 2021, www.livescience.com/does-every-star-have-planets.

90 Parker Solar Probe: "Parker Solar Probe: Humanity's First Visit to a Star," NASA, www. nasa.gov/content/goddard/parker-solar-probe-humanity-s-first-visit-to-a-star.

90 Alpha Centauri: Larry Sessions and Shireen Gonzaga, "Alpha Centauri: Star System Closest to Our Sun," EarthSky, April 7, 2021, earthsky.org/brightest-stars/alpha -centauri-is-the-nearest-bright-star.

CHAPTER 6: **E.T. PHONE HOME**

99 1936 broadcast: Ross Pomeroy, "Will Hitler Be the First Person That Aliens See?," *RealClearScience* (blog), September 20, 2013, www.realclearscience.com /blog/2013/09/will-hitler-be-the-first-person-that-aliens-see.html.

100 "If aliens visit us, the outcome": Stephen Hawking, *Stephen Hawking's Favorite Places*, directed by Ed Watkins, Bigger Bang / CuriosityStream, 2016.

101 Ants or chimpanzees: *The Twilight Zone*, season 5, episode 30, "Stopover in a Quiet Town," directed by Ron Winston, written by Earl Hamner Jr. and Rod Serling, aired April 24, 1964, on CBS.

103 Arecibo Message: Deborah Byrd, "The 1st Intentional Radio Message to Space Was Sent via Arecibo," EarthSky, November 20, 2020, earthsky.org/space/this -date-in-science-first-radio-signal-beamed-to-space.

104 Arecibo explainer: Arecibo Observatory, Britannica, www.britannica.com/topic /Arecibo-Observatory.

106 *Voyager*: "Mission Overview," NASA, voyager.jpl.nasa.gov/mission.

107 Golden Records: "The Golden Record," NASA, voyager.jpl.nasa.gov /golden-record.

107 *Voyager* in interstellar space: "Mission Status," NASA, voyager.jpl.nasa.gov /mission/status.

107 Scientists aren't sure how much longer the probes will last: Matthew Rozsa, "Humanity's Most Distant Spacecraft Is Sending Back Weird Signals from Beyond Our Solar System," *Salon*, May 23, 2022, www.salon.com/2022/05/23 /voyager-1-data.

109 Ad for tortilla chips: Colin Barras, "First Space Ad Targets Hungry Aliens," *New Scientist*, June 12, 2008, www.newscientist.com/article/dn14130-first-space -ad-targets-hungry-aliens.

111 Rosetta Stone: Foy Scalf, "The Rosetta Stone: Unlocking the Ancient Egyptian Language," American Research Center in Egypt, www.arce.org/resource /rosetta-stone-unlocking-ancient-egyptian-language.

111 AD 394: "Egyptian Hieroglyphs," Ancient Egypt Online, ancientegyptonline .co.uk/hieroglyphs.

112 *Beowulf* translation: "*Beowulf*—Opening Lines (1–11)," https://drmarkwomack .com/pdfs/beowulf-opening-lines.pdf.

113 Elephants' communication: Isabelle Dumé, "Elephants Turn to Seismic Communication," *Physics World*, June 8, 2004, physicsworld.com/a/elephants -turn-to-seismic-communication.

114 Zipf's law: Marc West, "The Mystery of Zipf," Plus, August 21, 2008, plus.maths .org/content/mystery-zipf.

115 Penguin communication: Bob Yirka, "Penguin Calls Found to Conform to Human Linguistic Laws," Phys.org, February 5, 2020, phys.org/news/2020-02-penguin -conform-human-linguistic-laws.html.

CHAPTER 7: **DO YOU BELIEVE IN ALIENS?**

118 San Luis Valley: Sarah Scoles, *They Are Already Here: UFO Culture and Why We See Saucers* (New York: Pegasus Books, 2020), 208.

124 Pueblo Indian legend: "Pueblo Indian Influences: Formative Period," Sangre de Cristo National Heritage Area, www.sangreheritage.org/formative.

127 Rare Earth Hypothesis: Doug Adler, "Rare Earth Hypothesis: Why We Might Really Be Alone in the Universe," *Astronomy*, July 29, 2022, astronomy.com /news/2022/07/rare-earth-hypothesis-why-we-might-really-be-alone-in-the -universe.

CHAPTER 8: **THE TRUTH IS OUT THERE**

132 2I/Borisov: "Interstellar Comet Borisov Reveals Its Chemistry and Possible Origins," *NASA*, April 20, 2020, www.nasa.gov/feature/interstellar-comet -borisov-reveals-its-chemistry-and-possible-origins.

132 Dr. Avi Loeb and 'Oumuamua: Lee Billings, "Astronomer Avi Loeb Says Aliens Have Visited, and He's Not Kidding," *Scientific American*, February 1, 2021, www .scientificamerican.com/article/astronomer-avi-loeb-says-aliens-have-visited -and-hes-not-kidding1.

133 Fermi Paradox: Elizabeth Howell, "Fermi Paradox: Where Are the Aliens?," Space .com, December 17, 2021, www.space.com/25325-fermi-paradox.html.

133 James Webb Space Telescope: See "NASA's Webb Delivers Deepest Infrared Image of Universe Yet," *NASA*, July 13, 2022, www.nasa.gov/image-feature /goddard/2022/nasa-s-webb-delivers-deepest-infrared-image-of-universe-yet.

136 James Webb Space Telescope explainer: "James Webb Space Telescope," NASA, webb.nasa.gov/index.html.

WHERE IS EVERYBODY?

140 Enceladus: Nancy Atkinson, "Meet Orbilander, a Mission to Search for Life on Enceladus," Planetary Society, October 8, 2020, www.planetary.org/articles /meet-orbilander-enceladus-mission.

140 Europa: "Europa: Jupiter's Ocean World," NASA Science, *last* updated June 27, 2019, spaceplace.nasa.gov/ikipe/en.

141 Mars: See Neel V. Patel, "The Best Places to Find Extraterrestrial Life in Our Solar System, Ranked," *MIT Technology Review*, June 16, 2021, www .technologyreview.com/2021/06/16/1026473/best-worlds-extraterrestrial -life-solar-system-ranked.

141 Titan: "Titan," NASA Science, last updated February 4, 2021, solarsystem.nasa. gov/moons/ikipe-moons/titan/in-depth.

142 Venus: Eric Verbeten, "Life Could Be Thriving in the Clouds of Venus," University of Wisconsin–Madison, January 6, 2022, news.wisc.edu/life-could-be-thriving -in-the-clouds-of-venus.

142 Pizza: Dominik Czernia and Kacper Pawlik, "Perfect Pizza Calculator," OMNI Calculator, April 6, 2022, www.omnicalculator.com/food/perfect-pizza.

142 TRAPPIST-1: Ed Browne, "James Webb Peers into TRAPPIST-1, a Star System Full of Earth-Like Planets," *Newsweek*, July 29, 2022, www.newsweek.com /james-webb-space-telescope-trappist-1-planets-life-1729236.

BIBLIOGRAPHY

BOOKS

Bennett, Jeffrey, and Seth Shostak. *Life in the Universe*. San Francisco: Pearson, 2016.

Dolnick, Edward. *The Writing of the Gods: The Race to Decode the Rosetta Stone*. New York: Scribner, 2021.

Fernades, Joaquim and Fina d'Armada. *Celestial Secrets: The Hidden History of the Fatima Cover-up*. Charlottesville, VA: Anomalist Books, 2007.

Kean, Leslie. *UFOs: Generals, Pilots, and Government Officials Go on the Record*. New York: Three Rivers Press, 2010.

Loeb, Avi. *Extraterrestrial: The First Sign of Intelligent Life Beyond Earth*. Boston: Mariner Books, 2022.

Scoles, Sarah. *They Are Already Here: UFO Culture and Why We See Saucers*. New York: Pegasus Books, 2020.

Shostak, Seth. *Confessions of an Alien Hunter: A Scientist's Search for Extraterrestrial Intelligence*. Washington, DC: National Geographic, 2009.

Ward, Peter D., and Donald Brownlee. *Rare Earth: Why Complex Life Is Uncommon in the Universe*. New York: Copernicus Books, 2003.

DOCUMENTARIES

Fox, James, dir. *I Know What I Saw*. 2009.

Watkins, Ed, dir. *Stephen Hawking's Favorite Places*. 2016.

TELEVISION

Winston, Ron, dir. "Stopover in a Quiet Town." Season 5, episode 30, *The Twilight Zone*. Aired April 24, 1964.

PERIODICALS

Adler, Doug. "Rare Earth Hypothesis: Why We Might Really Be Alone in the Universe." *Astronomy*, July 29, 2022. astronomy.com/news/2022/07/rare-earth-hypothesis-why-we-might-really-be-alone-in-the-universe.

Barras, Colin. "First Space Ad Targets Hungry Aliens." *New Scientist*, June 12, 2008. www.newscientist.com/article/dn14130-first-space-ad-targets-hungry-aliens.

Bialy, Shmuel, and Abraham Loeb. "Could Solar Radiation Pressure Explain 'Oumuamua's Peculiar Acceleration?" *Astrophysical Journal Letters*, November 20, 2018. iopscience.iop.org/article/10.3847/2041-8213/aaeda8/pdf.

Billings, Lee. "Astronomer Avi Loeb Says Aliens Have Visited, and He's Not Kidding." *Scientific American*, February 1, 2021. www.scientificamerican.com/article/astronomer -avi-loeb-says-aliens-have-visited-and-hes-not-kidding1.

Browne, Ed. "James Webb Peers into TRAPPIST-1, a Star System Full of Earth-Like Planets." *Newsweek*, July 29, 2022. See www.newsweek.com/james-webb-space -telescope-trappist-1-planets-life-1729236.

Cooper, Helene, Ralph Blumenthal, and Leslie Kean. "Glowing Auras and 'Black Money': The Pentagon's Mysterious U.F.O. Program." *New York Times*, December 16, 2017. www.nytimes.com/2017/12/16/us/politics/pentagon-program-ufo -harry-reid.html.

Davenport, Christian. "NASA Proved It Can Deflect an Asteroid. But Spotting Them Is Tricky." *Washington Post*, October 24, 2022. www.washingtonpost.com /technology/2022/10/24/nasa-asteroid-telescope/.

Dumé, Isabelle. "Elephants Turn to Seismic Communication." *Physics World*, June 8, 2004. physicsworld.com/a/elephants-turn-to-seismic-communication.

Fountain, Henry. "Two Trillion Galaxies, at the Very Least." *New York Times*, October 17, 2016. www.nytimes.com/2016/10/18/science/two-trillion-galaxies-at-the-very -least.html.

Johnson, Daniel. "Meet Proxima Centauri: The Closest Star." *Sky & Telescope*, November 30, 2021. skyandtelescope.org/astronomy-news/meet-proxima -centauri-closest-star.

Keilman, John. "'If We're Right, It Is the Biggest Secret in History': Chicago UFO Buffs Await Release of Pentagon Report into Unexplained Sightings." *Chicago Tribune*, June 22, 2021. www.chicagotribune.com/news/breaking/ct-ufo-report -chicago-flying-objects-20210622-nre2zkt7b5hj5ez3sb6ga4v7jq-story.html.

Lennon, Jay T., and Kenneth J. Locey. "There Are More Microbial Species on Earth Than Stars in the Galaxy." *Aeon*, September 10, 2018. aeon.co/ideas/there-are -more-microbial-species-on-earth-than-stars-in-the-sky.

Patel, Neel V. "The Best Places to Find Extraterrestrial Life in Our Solar System, Ranked." *MIT Technology Review*, June 16, 2021. See www.technologyreview. com/2021/06/16/1026473/best-worlds-extraterrestrial-life-solar-system-ranked.

Sooke, Alastair. "'If People Want Stonehenge to Be a UFO Landing Site, That's Fine.'" *Telegraph* (London). January 22, 2022. www.telegraph.co.uk/art/architecture /people-want-stonehenge-ufo-landing-site-fine.

Stothers, Richard. "Unidentified Flying Objects in Classical Antiquity." *Classical Journal* 103, no. 1 (2007). www.jstor.org/stable/30038660.

Walters, Sam. "Did Volcanic Eruptions Drive Dinosaurs to Extinction?" Discover, September 13, 2022. www.discovermagazine.com/the-sciences/did-volcanic -eruptions-drive-dinosaurs-to-extinction.

Yarwood, Vaughan. "X-Files: Strange Happenings in the South," *New Zealand Geographic*, July 2011. www.nzgeo.com/stories/x-files.

WEBSITES

"Anatomy of an Electromagnetic Wave." NASA Science. science.nasa.gov/ems /02_anatomy.

"Arecibo Observatory." Britannica. www.britannica.com/topic/Arecibo-Observatory.

"Asteroid." Britannica Kids. See kids.britannica.com/students/article/asteroid/272984.

"Asteroid or Meteor: What's the Difference?" NASA Science. spaceplace.nasa.gov /asteroid-or-meteor/en.

Atkinson, Nancy. "Meet Orbilander, a Mission to Search for Life on Enceladus." Planetary Society, October 8, 2020. www.planetary.org/articles/meet-orbilander -enceladus-mission.

Byrd, Deborah. "The 1st Intentional Radio Message to Space Was Sent via Arecibo." EarthSky, November 20, 2020. earthsky.org/space/this-date-in-science-first -radio-signal-beamed-to-space.

"Can Artificial Gravity Be Created in Space?" Ask an Astronomer. curious.astro.cornell
.edu/about-us/150-people-in-astronomy/space-exploration-and-astronauts
/general-questions/927-can-artificial-gravity-be-created-in-space-intermediate.

"Chemical Element." Britannica Kids. kids.britannica.com/kids/article/chemical
-element/352942.

Cooper, Keith. "Looking for LUCA, the Last Universal Common Ancestor." NASA,
March 30, 2017. astrobiology.nasa.gov/news/looking-for-luca-the-last-universal
-common-ancestor.

Czernia, Dominik, and Kacper Pawlik. "Perfect Pizza Calculator." OMNI Calculator,
April 6, 2022. www.omnicalculator.com/food/perfect-pizza.

David, Leonard. "UFOs Remain Elusive Despite Decades of Study." Space Insider,
Space.com, June 26, 2019. See www.space.com/ufo-investigations-mufon-50
-years.html.

"DNA." Britannica Kids. kids.britannica.com/kids/article/DNA/390730.

"DoD Announces the Establishment of the All-domain Anomaly Resolution Office."
U.S. Department of Defense, July 20, 2022. www.defense.gov/News/Releases
/Release/Article/3100053/dod-announces-the-establishment-of-the-all-domain
-anomaly-resolution-office.

"Does the Moon Have Gravity?" University of Southern Maine Planetarium. usm
.maine.edu/planet/does-moon-have-gravity.

"Egyptian Hieroglyphs." Ancient Egypt Online. ancientegyptonline.co.uk
/hieroglyphs.

"Electromagnetic Waves." BBC. www.bbc.co.uk/bitesize/guides/z9rqsrd
/revision/2.

"Europa: Jupiter's Ocean World." NASA *Science*, June 27, 2019. spaceplace
.nasa.gov/ikipe/en.

"Evolution." *Britannica Kids.* kids.britannica.com/students/article/evolution
/274236.

"The Evolution of the Telescope." Groovy Lab in a Box. www.groovylabinabox
.com/the-evolution-of-the-telescope.

"Fossil." Britannica Kids. See kids.britannica.com/students/article/fossil/274394.

"Galileo and the Telescope." Library of Congress. www.loc.gov/collections/finding
-our-place-in-the-cosmos-with-carl-sagan/articles-and-essays/modeling-the
-cosmos/galileo-and-the-telescope.

"Geologic Time Scale." CK–12 Foundation, last updated June 1, 2020. flexbooks
.ck12.org/cbook/ck-12-middle-school-life-science-2.0/section/4.12/primary
/lesson/timeline-of-evolution-ms-ls.

"The Golden Record." NASA. voyager.jpl.nasa.gov/golden-record.

Hamer, Ashley. "Does Every Star Have Planets?" Live Science, December 25, 2021.
www.livescience.com/does-every-star-have-planets.

"How Far Away Is the Moon?" Royal Museums Greenwich. www.rmg.co.uk/stories
/topics/how-far-away-moon.

"How Many Stars Are There in the Universe?" European Space Agency. www.esa
.int/Science_Exploration/Space_Science/Herschel/How_many_stars_are_there
_in_the_Universe.

"How Strong Is the Gravity on Jupiter?" CoolCosmos. coolcosmos.ipac.caltech
.edu/ask/93-How-strong-is-the-gravity-on-Jupiter-.

Howell, Elizabeth. "Fermi Paradox: Where Are the Aliens?" Space.com, December 17,
2021. www.space.com/25325-fermi-paradox.html.

Hunt, Katie, Ashley Strickland, and Jackie Wattles. "NASA Announces Team of
Scientists Who Will Study Mysterious 'UFO' Events in the Sky." CNN, October
24, 2022. www.cnn.com/2022/10/24/world/ufos-nasa-team-study-scn
/index.html.

"Interstellar Comet Borisov Reveals Its Chemistry and Possible Origins." NASA,
April 20, 2020. www.nasa.gov/feature/interstellar-comet-borisov-reveals-its
-chemistry-and-possible-origins.

"James Webb Space Telescope." NASA. webb.nasa.gov/index.html.

Jinkinson, Bethan. "10 Species Named After Famous People." BBC News, July 19,
2012. www.bbc.com/news/magazine-18889495.

Landau, Elizabeth. "What We Know—and Don't Know—About 'Oumuamua."
NASA Science, June 27, 2018. solarsystem.nasa.gov/news/473/what-we
-knowand-don't-knowabout-oumuamua.

Lee, Russell. "1947: Year of the Flying Saucer." National Air and Space Museum, June 24, 2022. airandspace.si.edu/stories/editorial/1947-year-flying-saucer.

"Light Speed." American Museum of Natural History. www.amnh.org/explore /ology/physics/train-of-thought2/light-speed.

Marker, Jonathan. "Public Interest in UFOs Persists 50 Years After Project Blue Book Termination." National Archives News, December 5, 2019. www.archives .gov/news/articles/project-blue-book-50th-anniversary.

Masetti, Maggie. "How Many Stars in the Milky Way Galaxy?" NASA Blueshift, June 22, 2015. asd.gsfc.nasa.gov/blueshift/index.php/2015/07/22/how -many-stars-in-the-milky-way.

Maydana, Sebastian. "Egyptian Pyramids That Are NOT in Giza (Top 10)." The Collector, January 20, 2022. www.thecollector.com/top-egyptian-pyramids.

"Men in Black." Wikipedia. en.wikipedia.org/wiki/Men_in_black.

"Mission Overview." NASA. voyager.jpl.nasa.gov/mission.

"Mission Status." NASA. voyager.jpl.nasa.gov/mission/status.

"NASA's Webb Delivers Deepest Infrared Image of Universe Yet." NASA, July 12, 2022. www.nasa.gov/image-feature/goddard/2022/nasa-s-webb-delivers-deepest -infrared-image-of-universe-yet.

"Occam's Razor." Academic Kids Encyclopedia. academickids.com/encyclopedia /index.php/Occam%27s_Razor.

"Pan-STARRS Across the Sky." NASA Science, April 5, 2019. science.nasa.gov/pan -starrs-across-sky.

"Parker Solar Probe: Humanity's First Visit to a Star." NASA. www.nasa.gov/content /goddard/parker-solar-probe-humanity-s-first-visit-to-a-star.

"Planetary Defense Coordination Office." NASA. www.nasa.gov/planetarydefense /overview.

Pomeroy, Ross. "Will Hitler Be the First Person That Aliens See?" *RealClearScience* (blog), September 20, 2013. www.realclearscience.com/blog/2013/09/will -hitler-be-the-first-person-that-aliens-see.html.

"Pueblo Indian Influences: Formative Period." Sangre de Cristo National Heritage Area. www.sangreheritage.org/formative.

"Pyramids of Giza." Britannica. www.britannica.com/place/Great-Pyramid-of-Giza.

"Roswell Incident." Britannica. www.britannica.com/event/Roswell-incident.

Rozsa, Matthew. "Humanity's Most Distant Spacecraft Is Sending Back Weird Signals from Beyond Our Solar System." Salon, May 23, 2022. www.salon.com/2022/05/23/voyager-1-data.

Scalf, Foy. "The Rosetta Stone: Unlocking the Ancient Egyptian Language." American Research Center in Egypt. www.arce.org/resource/rosetta-stone-unlocking-ancient-egyptian-language.

"Scientists Pinpoint How Many Planets in the Milky Way Could Host Life." Inverse, October 30, 2020. www.inverse.com/science/how-many-planets-host-life.

Sessions, Larry, and Shireen Gonzaga. "Alpha Centauri: Star System Closest to Our Sun." EarthSky, April 7, 2021. earthsky.org/brightest-stars/alpha-centauri-is-the-nearest-bright-star.

Shea, Marybeth. "Discovering Life in Yellowstone Where Nobody Thought It Could Exist." National Park Service. www.nps.gov/articles/thermophile-yell.htm.

Siegler, Ethan. "We Were Wrong: All Stars Don't Have Planets After All." Big Think, August 10, 2022. bigthink.com/starts-with-a-bang/stars-dont-have-planets.

Starr, Michele. "This Is the Last Full View the Kepler Spacecraft Saw Before It Shut Down Forever." Science Alert, February 7, 2017. www.sciencealert.com/this-is-the-last-full-view-the-kepler-spacecraft-saw-before-it-shut-down-forever.

Stephens, Tim. "Pioneering Radio Astronomer Frank Drake Dies at 92." UC Santa Cruz Newscenter, September 2, 2022. news.ucsc.edu/2022/09/frank-drake-in-memoriam.html.

Stolte, Daniel. "Mystery Peeled Off Banana Genome." University of Arizona News, July 12, 2012. news.arizona.edu/story/mystery-peeled-off-banana-genome.

"Titan." NASA Science, last updated February 4, 2021. solarsystem.nasa.gov/moons/saturn-moons/titan/in-depth.

Tobin, Taylor. "6 Ancient Sites That People Are Convinced Were Built by Aliens—and Why They Probably Weren't." Insider, July 2, 2018. www.insider.com/places-people-think-aliens-built-2018-7#the-nazca-lines-1.

"Tour of the Electromagnetic Spectrum." NASA Science. science.nasa.gov/ems/01_intro.

"UFO Sightings from Around the World." Artangel. www.artangel.org.uk/witness
    /ufo-sightings-from-around-world.

Verbeten, Eric. "Life Could Be Thriving in the Clouds of Venus." University of
    Wisconsin–Madison, January 6, 2022. news.wisc.edu/life-could-be-thriving-in
    -the-clouds-of-venus.

Water Science School. "The Water in You: Water and the Human Body." Water
    Science School, United States Geological Survey, May 22, 2019. www.usgs.gov
    /special-topics/water-science-school/science/water-you-water-and-human-body.

West, Marc. "The Mystery of Zipf." Plus, August 21, 2008. plus.maths.org/content
    /mystery-zipf.

"What Is Microgravity?" NASA, February 15, 2012. www.nasa.gov/audience
    /forstudents/5-8/features/nasa-knows/what-is-microgravity-58.html.

Wilson, Beth. "Staying in Shape in Space." Smithsonian, November 21, 2017.
    airandspace.si.edu/stories/editorial/staying-shape-space.

Womack, Mark. "Beowulf—Opening Lines (1–11)." https://drmarkwomack.com
    /pdfs/beowulf-opening-lines.pdf.

Yirka, Bob. "Penguin Calls Found to Conform to Human Linguistic Laws." Phys.org,
    February 5, 2020. phys.org/news/2020-02-penguin-conform-human-linguistic
    -laws.html.

ACKNOWLEDGMENTS

This book required the input of a galaxy's worth of people, starting with all the scientists, ufologists, and space nerds who shared their time, enthusiasm, and ideas with me. I'd especially like to acknowledge Dr. Frank Drake, who passed away as I was working on this book, and who inspired professional astronomers and amateur stargazers alike. A special shout-out to Dr. Jorge Perez-Gallego and to Dr. Sheri Wells-Jensen, who helped me keep my facts straight and suggested some excellent jokes. In addition, I'd like to thank Andrea Edwards and Miguel Boriss, both middle school science teachers who gave up precious summer time to read over the manuscript and make invaluable comments. Thanks, too, to Alicia Lincoln, who helped infuse this book with more wonder and clarity. A big thank-you to Laura Nolan, my literary agent, and to the wonderful people at Abrams Kids, who are a delight to collaborate with. I'm lucky to have Andrew Smith, Amy Vreeland, Ashley Albert, Kathy Lovisolo, Chelsea Hunter, and Hallie Patterson in my corner, and I'm luckier still to work with editor Howard Reeves and assistant editor Sara Sproull. A round of applause to Rafael Nobre, who once again created such beautiful illustrations. And another round to Richard Slovak, who made the copyediting process downright fun. Thank you to Sarah Scoles, with whom I will wax philosophical any day, especially if it involves being outside under the stars. Much love to Alison, Beth, and Kira, who cheered me on, long distance. I'm so grateful to my sister, Ashley, and my mom, Louise, for their support and to my dad, Chip, who is always happy to point his telescope at the night sky and share his awe about what's out there. But this book would not have been possible without the sun at the center of my solar system, my husband, Scott, whose constant love and energy infused this project with life and helped it flourish.

INDEX

Note: Page numbers in *italics* refer to illustrations.